NOT

JUST DESSERTS

Vegan / Gluten-Free Cooking

Jerry Weil

Introduction

In my last book, *Just Desserts,* I covered a variety of gluten/dairy-free desserts. As I was releasing it, I heard from a lot of people who asked about vegan options as well as foods other than desserts. I decided to begin working on this book, which covers sides, snacks, and entrees as well as desserts. Throughout the course of developing these recipes, I permanently changed my own diet; I am now completely vegan.

I tried not to duplicate too many recipes from the last book, and I also tried to avoid including vegan versions of non-vegan recipes in the first book; there are a few exceptions to that, but, for the most part these recipes are brand new. In the section about egg substitutes, I describe how to easily convert many recipes from *Just Desserts* into vegan recipes.

Egg Substitutes

There are many ways to substitute for eggs in vegan cooking. These days, there are more and more plant-based egg substitute products arriving in stores; I have not used these substitutes in my recipes, since they are fairly new and not readily available to everyone.

My main go to egg substitute is chia seeds. When you mix chia with water and let it sit for a few minutes, a gooey substance is formed which will bind foods in the way that eggs do. Using the whole seed this way does not appear very appetizing, so I first grind the seeds before using them in cooking; a coffee grinder is the best way to do this, but a food processor is the next best option. I also use white chia seeds (they are light brown when you grind them) – black seeds are not so attractive in your food. All of the cookie recipes from my first book, *Just Desserts,* can be made vegan by simply substituting the egg with a chia egg (1 Tbsp ground chia mixed with ¼ cup water, allowed to sit for a few minutes).

Another item which helps bind foods like eggs is xanthan gum. This is a common ingredient in gluten-free cooking, but I will sometimes include xanthan gum in recipes where I wouldn't have otherwise included it had I been using eggs (especially in cakes or muffins).

The final egg substitute I use is aquafaba; this is the liquid you find in a can of beans. I generally get my aquafaba from a can of garbanzo beans, but other beans can be used as well. This liquid makes a great substitute for egg whites; it even beats up just like egg whites if you add a little cream of tartar or xanthan gum.

Chocolate

I don't eat chocolate. Many people are allergic or have other sensitivities to chocolate. I find that carob is a great substitute, which gives a similar sensation to eating chocolate; I've had many people eat the desserts I make with carob and think they are eating chocolate. I always use unsweetened carob powder in my recipes, which can easily be substituted with unsweetened cocoa powder – one for one; so any of my carob desserts can be easily converted to chocolate with that one simple switch.

Honey

Though some vegans will not eat honey, I did include it in a couple of my recipes. You can always substitute something like agave, but keep in mind that honey is going to be thicker than most other liquid sweeteners. If it's something you're cooking, a different sweetener would need to be cooked down more to behave like honey.

Products

There are a few products on the market that I use in a lot of my recipes. These are very well established companies and products, and they should all be readily available in stores.

Earth Balance:	Their *buttery spread* product is the best vegan butter I have tried. It comes in several varieties, but I prefer using the soy-free version.
Daiya:	This company has a long history of vegan cheese products, which have always been soy-free and casein-free. They make a wide range of products, from frozen pizzas to cheesecake. Their most common product is their cheese shreds, and those are the products I use in the recipes in this book.
Beyond Meat:	This is a fairly new company in the marketplace, and they have a growing assortment of plant-based meat substitutes. Some recipes in this book make use of their crumbles, which make an excellent ground beef substitute.
Coconut Aminos:	This is a great substitute for soy sauce. I try not to eat soy (unless it's fermented), and not only is this product soy-free, but it also has a little natural coconut sweetness.
Coconut Nectar:	Yes, I do love coconut, and there are so many great products made from coconuts. This is a great sweetener, and I use just a little bit in many of my dishes. You could also substitute maple syrup if you don't have any in your kitchen.

Tools

There are some basic tools which are necessary for some of my recipes. You can work your way around some of them, but some are fairly inexpensive and will save you a lot of time in the kitchen.

Food Processor:	This is really a must for many of my recipes. I highly recommend the **Ninja**, which is fairly inexpensive at **Target**. Aside from grinding and pureeing, I use it for some chopping as well (especially onions or nuts).

Large Skillet (with lid):	This item is not cheap, but once you have one you will use it all the time. Having a lid is so useful; you then have the option of letting the liquid cook off or stay in the pan, depending on whether you have the lid off or on. I probably use this more than any other pot or pan in my kitchen.
Steamer:	I like to steam vegetables whenever possible – it's really easy to do, and will maintain more of the vitamins and nutrients than other forms of cooking. The cheap way to go is to use a basket, which will fit into a regular pot. I prefer to use the steamer insert, which is like a double boiler with holes in the bottom.
Pastry Bag:	This may seem like something too fancy for most people, but once you have one you will use it all the time. It's inexpensive, and after buying a bag, you can buy new tips as needed.
Silicone Baking Mat:	This is only mandatory for one of my recipes, but it's a great thing to have on hand. It's fully washable and reusable, and makes a great non-stick surface for your cookies and pastries. It also won't transfer the heat from the metal as much as parchment paper, so the bottoms won't burn. I still tend to use parchment paper most of the time, but I like having this around when I need it.
Squeeze Bottles:	These simple, inexpensive, plastic bottles will make your dishes look professional. You can use them to apply sauces, syrups, or glazes in decorative patterns.

Difficulty Ratings

As in the first book, I have included a rating system for each recipe. Next to the name is a number between [1] and [5]; 1 is the easiest, 5 is the hardest. A level [1] rating is for recipes that call for simply combining ingredients. Level [5] recipes tend to include difficult steps that will take some practice to master. Most of the recipes in this book tend to lie in the [2] to [3] range.

Table of Contents

ALMOND CRACKERS [3]

I have included this one version of a cracker, but there are endless possibilities of other flavors. Try other flours and flavorings, and have fun!

INGREDIENTS

¼ cup almond flour
¼ cup brown rice flour
¼ cup tapioca flour (plus extra for rolling out)
¼ tsp xanthan gum
1 tsp sugar
½ tsp chopped parsley
½ tsp chopped basil
¼ tsp salt
2 tsp oil
¼ cup water

PREPARATION

1) Preheat oven to 400 degrees
2) In a mixing bowl, combine dry ingredients.
3) Add oil, and mix well.
4) Add water, and mix to form a dough. Work the dough for a couple of minutes with your hands until smooth.
5) Cover a baking sheet with parchment paper, and cover the ball of dough with tapioca flour.
6) Press dough onto center of baking sheet to form a rectangle. Place a sheet of wax paper on top, and roll out to desired thickness. Try to maintain dough as rectangular as possible.
7) Prick dough with a fork to prevent air pockets.
8) With a pastry cutter, cut dough vertically at 1 ½ inch intervals. Do the same in the horizontal direction.
9) Bake for 12-14 minutes, until crackers begin to brown slightly. If some sections brown quicker, remove them and continue baking. Makes around 3 dozen.

BREAD [3]

This is a basic bread, which is a good place to start. From here, you can add different spices, nuts, or dried fruit to create other flavors. Save the crumbs when you slice it, and use them in other recipes that call for bread crumbs.

INGREDIENTS

1 ½ cups water
¼ cup sugar
3 packets active dry yeast
2 Tbsp ground chia
¼ cup water
1/3 cup oil
2 tsp apple cider vinegar
1 ½ cups brown rice flour
1 ½ cups millet flour
2 ½ cups tapioca flour
1 tsp xanthan gum
½ tsp salt

PREPARATION

1) Place water and sugar in a medium saucepan. Heat to 105-115 degrees, stirring until sugar is dissolved.
2) Sprinkle yeast on top. Shake pan just until all yeast is covered with liquid. Let sit for 15-20 minutes – contents will more than double in size.
3) Meanwhile, place chia and water in a large bowl. Mix and let sit for 5 minutes or until a thick paste is formed. Stir in oil and vinegar.
4) Combine remaining dry ingredients separately, then add to the chia mixture. Mix thoroughly.
5) Form a well in the center, and pour in the yeast mixture. Mix well, then stir vigorously until a very thick batter is formed.
6) Turn batter into a bread pan which has been sprayed with oil. Even out dough in pan.
7) Cover pan with a large inverted bowl (you can use a towel, but it's better to cover with something that leaves room for dough to rise). Let dough rise for one hour.
8) Preheat oven to 375 degrees. Bake bread for 50-55 minutes, or until center reaches over 200 degrees. Cool and slice.

PANCAKES [2]

This is a great breakfast that everyone loves. I like to top with a homemade blueberry syrup, but plain maple syrup works great too.

INGREDIENTS

2 Tbsp ground chia seeds
½ cup water
½ cup millet flour
½ cup brown rice flour
½ cup arrowroot starch
4 tsp baking powder
½ tsp cinnamon
1 cup almond milk
2 tsp Earth Balance

PREPARATION

1) Mix chia and water. Let sit for a few minutes until thick.
2) Add remaining ingredients except Earth Balance, and mix well.
3) Heat a skillet over medium heat.
4) Melt ¼ tsp Earth Balance in skillet, and swirl around to coat bottom.
5) Pour ¼ cup of batter into center of skillet, and shake the skillet to spread batter.
6) When bottom turns golden, turn over with a spatula. Cook other side until golden.
7) Repeat until all batter is used. Makes 8 pancakes.

APPLE LIME CREPES [3]

You can use any filling you like for these delicious crepes – here's one winning combination.

INGREDIENTS

Crepes
2 Tbsp ground chia seeds
½ cup water
½ cup millet flour
½ cup brown rice flour
½ cup arrowroot starch
¼ tsp xanthan gum
1 1/2 cups almond milk
8 tsp Earth Balance

Filling
4 medium apples (peeled, cored, and chopped)
3 Tbsp lime juice
½ cup agave
1 tsp cinnamon

Topping
2 Tbsp powdered sugar

PREPARATION

1) Make filling by placing all ingredients into a saucepan. Stir together and cook over low heat until apples are soft (about 20 minutes).
2) For the crepes, mix chia and water in a mixing bowl. Let sit for a few minutes until thick.
3) Add remaining ingredients except Earth Balance, and mix well.
4) Heat a skillet over medium heat.
5) Melt 1 tsp Earth Balance in skillet, and swirl around to coat bottom.
6) Pour ¼ cup – 1/3 cup of batter into center of skillet, and shake the skillet to spread batter. Use a fork to spread the batter as thinly as possible without leaving holes.
7) Raise heat on skillet and cook until bottom of crepe starts to form brown spots.
8) Turn crepe and cook until second side starts to brown. Place crepe on a plate and lower heat back to medium heat; let skillet cool slightly before cooking next crepe.
9) For each crepe, spread 1/8 of the filling on one side of the crepe; Roll crepe and place seam side down on the plate;
10) Dust crepes with powdered sugar. Makes 8.

WAFFLES [1]

Waffles are a really easy and great breakfast. A good Belgian waffle iron makes all the difference - I recommend getting one which flips over.

INGREDIENTS

2 Tbsp ground chia seeds
½ cup water
1 cup millet flour
1 cup brown rice flour
1 cup tapioca flour
4 tsp baking powder
½ tsp xanthan gum
2 cups almond milk

PREPARATION

1) Mix chia and water. Let sit for a few minutes until thick.
2) Add remaining ingredients and mix well. Stir vigorously for a few seconds.
3) After heating iron, spray with oil (even if it's non-stick). Pour enough batter onto iron to just fill to the edges. Cook for around 5 minutes. Makes 4 large Belgian waffles.

FRENCH TOAST [2]

The quality of the bread makes all the difference – bake your own bread for best results! A non-stick pan makes this much easier, but any pan will do as long as you frequently loosen the toast to keep it from sticking.

INGREDIENTS

4 slices vegan/gluten-free bread
2 Tbsp ground chia seeds
½ cup water
¼ cup almond milk
¼ tsp cinnamon

PREPARATION

1) Slice bread in half.
2) Place chia and water in a bowl. Mix and let sit for 5 minutes to thicken.
3) Add almond milk, and mix well. Add cinnamon, and swirl it around – don't completely blend it in.
4) Add enough oil to a skillet to fully coat, and heat over medium heat.
5) One by one, dip each piece of bread in the batter to fully coat, and add to the skillet. When the bottom is browned, turn over to brown other side.
6) Place cooked toast on a paper towel to drain. Top with powdered sugar and maple syrup. Serves 2.

CEREAL [2]

For years I would make a special trip to one store that carried a cereal similar to this. One week they were out of it, so I decided to make it myself; now I make it all the time, and it's nice to be able to change it up with different ingredients. You can experiment with different dried fruit, nuts, and seeds.

INGREDIENTS

½ cup quinoa
½ cup water
½ cup medjool dates (pitted)
½ cup raisins
1 apple (peeled, cored, and coarsely chopped)
1 banana
½ cup pecans
½ cup sunflower seeds
¼ cup chia seeds
1 tsp cinnamon

PREPARATION

1) In a pot, mix quinoa with water. Cook over low heat until water is absorbed.
2) Preheat oven to 170 degrees.
3) Place all fruit in a food processor and blend until smooth. Pour into a bowl.
4) Place quinoa and remaining ingredients in a food processor, and pulse until coarsely ground and well mixed.
5) Add dry mixture to fruit mixture, and mix well to form a paste.
6) Cover a cookie sheet with parchment paper, and spread paste on paper. Use a knife to spread and shape into a rectangle which is about 1/8 inch thick and as even as possible.
7) Bake for around 6 hours or to desired hardness. Cereal will get crisper as it cools, so don't let it get too hard. Outside will bake faster, so periodically break off outside edges as they become ready. Break into bite size pieces. Makes 6-8 servings.

CHIA OMELETTE [2]

No one will be fooled to think this is made with real eggs, but it's a great, healthy alternative.

INGREDIENTS

2 Tbsp ground chia seeds
½ cup water
2 Tbsp brown rice flour
1 tsp nutritional yeast
1/8 tsp baking powder
¼ tsp tarragon
¼ tsp parsley
Pinch turmeric
Salt and pepper to taste
1 Tbsp Earth Balance
½ cup chopped vegetables
2 Tbsp Daiya cheese shreds

PREPARATION

1) Place chia and water in a bowl. Mix, and let sit for 5 minutes to thicken.
2) Add flour, yeast, baking powder, and spices, and mix well.
3) Heat a skillet over medium heat. Add Earth Balance and melt to cover pan. Add chia mixture and continue cooking over medium heat – it will take a lot longer to cook than eggs do.
4) Meanwhile, pour a little oil in another pan, and lightly sauté the vegetables.
5) Once omelette is fully cooked on the bottom, flip with a spatula. Add the vegetables to the center and top with cheese.
6) Once bottom of omelette is fully cooked, fold over ends and flip skillet onto a plate. Makes one omelette.

CINNAMON RAISIN BAGELS[4]

There's nothing like a freshly made bagel. Toast these and spread some Daiya cream cheese on top.

INGREDIENTS

1 ½ cups water

4 Tbsp sugar

2 packets active dry yeast

1 tsp cinnamon

1 ¼ cup brown rice flour

1 ¼ cup millet flour

2 cups tapioca flour
            (plus extra for working dough)

1 tsp xanthan gum

½ cup raisins

PREPARATION

1) In a saucepan, combine 1 Tbsp sugar and water; heat to 105-115 degrees. Sprinkle yeast on top and swirl pan until the yeast is all covered. Let sit for 15 minutes (will more than double in volume).

2) In a small bowl, combine remaining sugar and cinnamon. Set aside.

3) In a large bowl, combine remaining ingredients except raisins. Make a well in the center and pour in the yeast mixture. Stir vigorously until a soft dough is formed. Mix in raisins. Add extra starch until dough is not too sticky.

4) Sprinkle cinnamon and sugar mixture on top of dough. Fold and knead dough until all sugar is incorporated.

5) Place dough in a clean bowl lined with plastic wrap. Cover the bowl with more plastic wrap, and let dough rise for 45 minutes (should double in size).

6) Preheat oven to 400 degrees.

7) Lightly flour a large piece of wax paper with tapioca flour. Break dough into eight pieces. Roll each piece into a ball, and place on the wax paper (Leave plenty of room for spreading). Push the center down with your thumb; Flour the top, then turn over and push down center from the other side to form a bagel shape. Cover bagels with plastic wrap, and let rise for another 10 minutes.

8) Bring a large pot of water to a boil. Carefully place each bagel into the water and boil for 1 minute on each side. Don't boil more than three at a time so there is enough room for the bagels. Place boiled bagels on a cookie sheet covered with parchment paper.

9) Bake bagels for 20 minutes, then turn the bagels over and bake for another 5 minutes. They are best eaten sliced and toasted with your favorite toppings; I recommend Earth Balance or Daiya cream cheese.

CINNAMON ROLLS[4]

These are great for breakfast, but they also make a great dessert!

INGREDIENTS

Dough
½ cup almond milk
¼ cup sugar
2 packets active dry yeast
1 Tbsp ground chia seeds
¼ cup water
1/3 cup Earth Balance
1 cup brown rice flour
1 cup millet flour
½ tsp xanthan gum
½ cup tapioca flour (plus extra for rolling out)

Filling
¼ cup Earth Balance
½ cup pecans
½ cup sugar
1 Tbsp cinnamon

Glaze
1 cup powdered sugar
1 tsp vanilla extract
2 Tbsp almond milk

PREPARATION

1) To make the dough, place sugar and almond milk into a small saucepan. Heat to between 105 and 115 degrees, stirring so the sugar is dissolved.
2) Sprinkle yeast over the surface of the saucepan, swirling the pan just enough so the liquid covers all the yeast. Let sit for around 15 minutes.
3) Meanwhile, place ground chia and water into a large bowl and let sit until thick.
4) Cream Earth Balance into chia mixture.
5) Combine remaining dry ingredients except tapioca flour, and add to the chia and Earth Balance mixture. Mix until well integrated. Form a well in the center.
6) Add yeast mixture, and stir vigorously until a soft dough is formed.
7) Work in tapioca flour a little at a time, only until the dough does not stick to your hands. Use extra if necessary.
8) Flour a large sheet of wax paper with tapioca flour, in an area approximately 15 X 12 inches.
9) Using your hands, press the dough onto the wax paper and shape to a rectangle which is 15 X 12 inches.
10) For the filling, melt Earth Balance and brush evenly over the surface of the dough.
11) Place pecans in a food processor and pulse until finely chopped. Combine with sugar and cinnamon, and sprinkle evenly on top of the melted Earth Balance.
12) Lift the edge of the wax paper and use to push the dough onto itself, rolling into a 15 inch long roll.
13) Spray a 9X13 inch pan with oil. Using a sharp knife, slice one inch slices from the roll and place flat side down into the pan; shape the slices as round as possible, and butt them next to each other in a 5 column, 3 row grid. Flatten the slices slightly with the palm of your hand.
14) Cover the pan with a cloth, and allow the dough to rise for about one hour.
15) Preheat oven to 350 degrees.
16) Bake rolls for 30 minutes.
17) When rolls are mostly cooled, make glaze by adding vanilla extract and almond milk to the powdered sugar; stir until smooth, and spread evenly on top of the rolls.
18) Once glaze hardens, cut or tear rolls apart. Makes 15.

BLUEBERRY MUFFINS[2]

Great as breakfast, a snack, or even dessert.

INGREDIENTS

3 Tbsp chia seeds
¾ cup water
2 medium apples
1 cup sugar
¼ cup oil
1 tsp apple cider vinegar
¾ cup brown rice flour
½ cup millet flour
¾ cup arrowroot starch
1 Tbsp baking powder
½ tsp baking soda
¼ tsp xanthan gum
½ cup blueberries

PREPARATION

1) Preheat oven to 375 degrees
2) In a large mixing bowl, combine chia seeds and water. Let sit for a few minutes. Stir.
3) Peel and core apples. Coarsely chop them, and place in a food processor. Pulse in processor to finely chop the apples.
4) Add chopped apples and remaining ingredients except blueberries, and mix well. Stir vigorously for 30 seconds to activate xanthan gum.
5) Mix in blueberries.
6) Place muffin cups in a muffin pan, and fill to the top with batter.
7) Let sit for 5 minutes.
8) Bake for 25-30 minutes, or until a toothpick comes out clean. Makes one dozen.

BANANA NUT MUFFINS[2]

You can never have too many varieties of muffins, so here's another alternative.

INGREDIENTS

3 Tbsp chia seeds
¾ cup water
3 large bananas (mashed)
1 cup medjool dates (chopped)
¼ cup oil
1 cup brown rice flour
½ cup almond flour
½ cup arrowroot starch
1 Tbsp baking powder
½ tsp baking soda
¼ tsp xanthan gum
1 cup walnuts (chopped)

PREPARATION

1) Preheat oven to 375 degrees
2) In a large mixing bowl, combine chia seeds and water. Let sit for a few minutes. Stir.
3) Add remaining ingredients except walnuts, and mix well. Stir vigorously for 30 seconds to activate xanthan gum.
4) Mix in walnuts.
5) Place muffin cups in a muffin pan, and fill to the top with batter.
6) Let sit for 5 minutes.
7) Bake for 25-30 minutes, or until a toothpick comes out clean. Makes one dozen.

CHERRY TURNOVERS[3]

I love it when cherries are in season. You can use other fruit for the filling as well. I've experimented with making vegan, gluten-free puff pastry, but not had much success. This is a simplified version which won't give you that flaky texture, but it still tastes great.

INGREDIENTS

Dough
1 Tbsp ground chia
¼ cup water
½ cup Earth Balance
3 Tbsp sugar
½ cup millet flour
½ cup brown rice flour
½ cup tapioca flour (plus extra for rolling out)
1 tsp baking powder
½ tsp xanthan gum

Filling
2 cups cherries (pitted)
¼ cup brown rice syrup
1 Tbsp arrowroot starch

Frosting
½ cup powdered sugar
2 Tbsp almond milk

PREPARATION

1) In a bowl, combine chia and water. Let sit for a few minutes until thick.
2) Cream Earth Balance and sugar into the chia mixture.
3) Add remaining dough ingredients and mix well. Stir vigorously to form a soft dough. If dough is sticky, add more tapioca flour. Form a ball of dough, and chill for 30 minutes.
4) While dough is chilling, make filling by placing cherries and rice syrup in a saucepan. Heat over medium heat, stirring occasionally, for 10-15 minutes.
5) Flatten cherries with a fork. Mix in arrowroot starch; continue cooking for another minute, stirring constantly. Remove from heat.
6) Preheat oven to 375 degrees.
7) Cover a piece of wax paper with tapioca flour. Cover dough with flour, and press onto the center of the paper, shaping into a rectangle.
8) Flour the top of the dough, and place another piece of wax paper on top. Roll out to 1/8 inch thickness.
9) Use a pastry cutter to cut into 3 inch squares. Place squares onto a cookie sheet covered with parchment paper (use a spatula to transfer the squares). Roll out left over dough until all dough has been used.
10) Place 1 Tbsp filling onto the center of each square, and fold them in half diagonally; press edges together to seal pastries.
11) Bake for 30 minutes, or until edges are browned.
12) Once pastries have cooled, mix frosting by combining all ingredients until smooth. With pastries on parchment paper or wax paper, drizzle frosting on top. Allow frosting to harden. Makes 16.

APPLE STRUDEL[5]

One of the more difficult pastries to make, but well worth it. The most difficult part is the rolling up of the strudel, so go slowly and carefully.

INGREDIENTS

Dough

¼ cup Earth Balance
2 Tbsp sugar
½ cup brown rice flour
½ cup millet flour
½ cup tapioca flour (plus extra for rolling out)
½ tsp xanthan gum
6 Tbsp water

Filling

½ cup raisins
3 Tbsp rum
1/3 cup gluten free bread crumbs
¼ cup + 1 tsp Earth Balance
½ cup sugar
1 Tbsp cinnamon
½ lb apples
Juice of ½ lemon

PREPARATION

1) Make the dough by creaming Earth Balance with sugar until smooth.
2) Combine remaining dry ingredients separately, then add to the Earth Balance mixture. Mix well.
3) Mix in water a little at a time, until a very soft dough is formed – it should be fairly sticky. Stir vigorously until it holds together well.
4) Work in a little more tapioca flour, until the dough is no longer sticky.
5) Chill dough while filling is being prepared.
6) Mix raisins and rum in a bowl, and set aside.
7) Melt 1 tsp Earth balance in a skillet, and mix in the bread crumbs; cook until crumbs are dry and toasted.
8) In a bowl, mix toasted bread crumbs with sugar and cinnamon.
9) Melt remaining ¼ cup Earth Balance and set aside.
10) Peel and core the apples. Chop them finely, and mix with lemon juice. Add raisins to the apples and mix.
11) Preheat oven to 350 degrees.
12) Place a large piece of wax paper on a flat surface, and flour it generously with tapioca flour. Dip the chilled dough in the starch, and press down onto the center of the paper to form a long rectangle.
13) Flour the top of the dough, and place another piece of wax paper on top. Gently roll out dough, periodically removing paper to make sure it's not sticking to the dough – if it is, add more flour and continue rolling out. Maintain as squared off of a rectangle as possible by adjusting with your hands. Roll out to approximately 10" X 16".
14) Brush the top of the dough with half the melted Earth Balance. Sprinkle bread crumb mixture on top, leaving a one inch edge all around.
15) Cover crumbs evenly with apple mixture. Press apple mixture down lightly with your hands.
16) Using the wax paper as a guide, fold the bottom and top edges on top of the apples. Press the dough down gently.
17) Cover a cookie sheet with parchment paper, and place it to the left to form a continuous surface with the wax paper. Using the wax paper as a guide, fold the right edge of the dough onto the apples. Press the dough down lightly. Push the dough with the paper to roll right to left. Go slowly and carefully to avoid any tearing of the dough. Roll the strudel onto the cookie sheet, seam side down. Adjust the dough with your hands as needed to form an even roll.
18) Brush the outside of the dough with remaining melted Earth Balance. Bake for 40 minutes. Cool and slice.

BEIGNETS[3]

These are baked, not fried, and they still taste delicious. They go great with a cup of coffee.

INGREDIENTS

½ cup + 2 Tbsp water
2 Tbsp sugar
1 packet active dry yeast
1 Tbsp ground chia
2 Tbsp water
2 Tbsp Earth Balance (melted)
1 tsp apple cider vinegar
1 tsp vanilla extract
½ cup brown rice flour
½ cup millet flour
½ cup tapioca flour (+ extra for working dough)
½ tsp xanthan gum

PREPARATION

1) Place ½ cup water and sugar in a medium saucepan. Heat to 105-115 degrees, stirring until sugar is dissolved.
2) Sprinkle yeast on top. Shake pan just until all yeast is covered with liquid. Let sit for 15-20 minutes – contents will more than double in size.
3) Meanwhile, place chia and 2 Tbsp water in a large bowl. Mix and let sit for 5 minutes or until a thick paste is formed. Stir in half the melted Earth Balance, vinegar, and vanilla.
4) Combine remaining dry ingredients separately, then add to the chia mixture. Mix thoroughly.
5) Form a well in the center, and pour in the yeast mixture. Mix well, then stir vigorously until a soft dough is formed. Dough should be a little sticky, but should not stick to your hands – if it does, add more tapioca flour until it no longer sticks.
6) Line a clean bowl with plastic wrap. Place the dough on top, then cover the bowl with more plastic wrap. Let dough rise for one hour.
7) Cover a cookie sheet with parchment paper, and sprinkle a little tapioca flour in the center. Flip the dough on top of the paper, and sprinkle more flour on top of the dough. Roll out to a 6 X 6 inch square, using your hands to help shape the square.
8) Cut the dough into 1 ½ inch squares with a pastry cutter. Separate the squares to leave some room for spreading.
9) Cover with a damp towel, and let rise for another 45 minutes. Preheat oven to 350 degrees.
10) Bake for about 13 minutes. Brush with the remaining melted Earth Balance.
11) Dust with powdered sugar, or place in a bag with the sugar and shake the bag to coat the beignets. Best served warm. Makes 16.

CHURROS[3]

These churros are baked, not fried. They will go stale pretty quickly, so you'll have to eat them while they're fresh!

INGREDIENTS

1 Tbsp ground chia seeds
1 ¼ cups water
1 tsp vanilla extract
1 Tbsp Earth Balance
2 Tbsp sugar
½ cup brown rice flour
½ cup millet flour
2 Tbsp tapioca flour
¼ tsp xanthan gum

Topping
1 Tbsp Earth Balance
3 Tbsp sugar
½ tsp cinnamon

PREPARATION

1) Preheat oven to 350 degrees.
2) In a small bowl, combine the ground chia and ¼ cup water. Let sit for 5 minutes, until mixture gets thick. Mix in vanilla extract.
3) Place remaining water, Earth Balance, and sugar in a saucepan. Heat until Earth Balance is melted, then bring contents to a boil.
4) Meanwhile, combine remaining ingredients. Once the contents of the saucepan is boiling, lower heat and add combined dry ingredients all at once. Whisk together until dough is smooth.
5) Remove from heat, and whisk in chia mixture. Combine until smooth. Place dough in a pastry bag with a large star tip.
6) Cover a baking sheet with parchment paper. Pipe 4 inch strips of dough onto the paper.
7) Bake for 30-35 minutes, until golden and crunchy. Let cool.
8) For the topping, melt the Earth Balance. Brush churros with the melted butter.
9) Combine sugar and cinnamon. Roll the churros in the mixture. Makes around 30.

LENTIL BURGERS[4]

Everything is home made, so it's a bit of work. I use black lentils because they look like ground beef, but other lentils could be used as well – be sure to adjust the amount of water for the type of bean; smaller beans (like red lentils) require less water.

INGREDIENTS

Buns

1 ½ cups water
1 Tbsp sugar
2 packets active dry yeast
1 Tbsp ground chia seeds
1 cup brown rice flour
1 cup millet flour
2 cups tapioca flour
½ tsp xanthan gum
¼ cup oil

Burgers

1 cup black lentils
3 ½ cups water
1 Tbsp ground chia seeds
¼ cup water
2 cups cooked brown rice
3 Tbsp coconut aminos
1 Tbsp oil
¼ cup tapioca flour

Ketchup

8 roma tomatoes (cored, peeled, and coarsely chopped)
¼ cup vinegar
3 Tbsp coconut nectar
1 tsp salt
1 tsp mustard powder

PREPARATION

1) To make the buns, heat 1 ¼ cups of water and the sugar in a saucepan to between 105 and 115 degrees. Mix until sugar is dissolved.
2) Sprinkle yeast on top of water, and shake pan until yeast is covered with the water. Let set for 15 minutes.
3) Meanwhile, combine chia and remaining ¼ cup water. Let sit for 5 minutes until thick.
4) Separately combine dry ingredients, and combine with the chia mixture. Add oil and mix well.
5) Make a well in the center, and add the yeast mixture. Stir vigorously to form a soft dough. Work in extra tapioca flour if too sticky.
6) Cover a baking sheet with parchment paper. Divide the dough into 8 pieces, and roll each into a smooth ball. Place on the baking sheet spaced well apart. Cover with a large inverted baking dish and let rise for 1 hour.
7) Preheat oven to 425 degrees.
8) Bake buns for 10 minutes. Cool, and slice in half.
9) To make the patties, rinse and sort lentils. Place in a saucepan with water, lid tilted. Cook over medium heat until water is all absorbed – around 40-50 minutes. Stir occasionally so beans don't burn.
10) Combine chia and water in a bowl, and let sit for 5 minutes until thick.
11) Preheat oven to 350 degrees.
12) Add cooked lentils and remaining ingredients. Mix well.
13) Form into 8 patties. Place on a cookie sheet covered with parchment paper.
14) Bake for 10 minutes on each side.
15) For Ketchup, place all ingredients in a food processor; grind until smooth. Pour into a saucepan and cook over low heat until thick (1 – 1 ½ hours).
16) I recommend lightly toasting the bun halves. Makes 8 burgers.

MATZO BALL SOUP [3]

This is a great starter to a Passover meal, but it's delicious any time of year.

INGREDIENTS

Soup
2 Tbsp oil
1 onion
2 tsp crushed garlic
2 stalks celery
2 carrots
3 cups vegetable broth
3 cups water
1 tsp dill
1 tsp chopped parsley

Matzo Balls
2 Tbsp ground chia seeds
½ cup water
1 ½ cups almond flour
1/3 cup tapioca flour
½ tsp baking soda
½ tsp salt

Jack Fruit (optional)
½ can jack fruit
2 Tbsp oil
2 Tbsp coconut aminos
1 tsp sage

PREPARATION

1) Make matzo balls by combining chia and water; let sit for a few minutes until thick.
2) Add remaining ingredients to chia mixture and mix well to form a sticky dough.
3) Cover dough with plastic wrap and chill until ready to add to soup.
4) For soup, heat oil in a large pot. Finely chop onion (or grind in a food processor). Cook in oil over medium heat until golden, stirring often to keep from burning (about 20 minutes).
5) Add crushed garlic, and cook for 2-3 minutes more.
6) Add remaining ingredients. Bring to a boil, then continue to simmer covered for 30 minutes.
7) Break off 1 inch balls of dough. Roll with your hands until smooth, and place on a piece of wax paper. Once all balls are made, drop into simmering soup. Should make approximately 15.
8) With lid on the pot, continue to simmer for 30 minutes.
9) While soup is simmering, prepare the jack fruit by first washing and draining the fruit.
10) Heat oil in a skillet, and add the fruit. Sautee until soft (about 5-10 minutes).
11) Crush the pieces of fruit with the back of a fork, add coconut aminos, and continue cooking for another 5 minutes.
12) Add sage and cook until all liquid is gone.
13) Once soup is finished cooking, stir in the jack fruit. Makes 4-5 servings.

CHILE [2]

The Beyond Meat crumbles are so good, you might fool non-vegans into thinking they are eating meat!

INGREDIENTS

1/3 cup Earth Balance
1 medium onion (finely chopped)
1 Tbsp crushed garlic
1 lb Beyond Meat beef crumbles (Feisty)
2 Tbsp cumin
2 Tbsp chile powder
2 tsp paprika
2 tsp cinnamon
1 tsp turmeric
1 tsp salt
4 cups diced roma tomatoes
1 green pepper (chopped)
1 red pepper (chopped)
2 15 oz cans kidney beans
¼ cup coconut nectar

PREPARATION

1) In a large pot, melt Earth Balance over medium heat. Add chopped onion and cook for 20 to 30 minutes, stirring frequently. Onions should be browned.
2) Add crushed garlic, and cook for 2-3 minutes more.
3) Add beef crumbles and spices, stir together, and cook for 3-5 minutes.
4) Add tomatoes and peppers, and stir until well mixed. Cook uncovered for about 1 hour, stirring occasionally. Tomatoes should be completely broken down, and consistency should be fairly thick.
5) Drain kidney beans, and add to the chile mixture. Stir well, and continue cooking for 20 – 30 minutes, or until desired consistency.
6) Serve with crumbled almond crackers (page 11) and Daiya cheddar shreds. Serves 4-6.

BROCCOLI SOUP[1]

A very simple, great tasting soup. And great for St. Patrick's Day!

INGREDIENTS

3 Tbsp Earth Balance
½ onion (chopped)
1 large head of broccoli (chopped)
1 apple (peeled, cored, and chopped)
2 cups vegetable broth
1 cup water
1 Tbsp coconut nectar (optional)
½ cup mushrooms (chopped)
½ cup parlsey (chopped)
Salt and pepper to taste
½ cup coconut milk beverage

PREPARATION

1) In a large saucepan, melt Earth Balance over medium heat. Add chopped onion and cook for 2 minutes.
2) Add broccoli and apple, stir, and cook covered for 30 minutes.
3) Cool slightly, then place into food processor and process until smooth. Return to pot and add broth, water, coconut nectar, mushrooms, parsley, salt, and pepper. Bring to a boil, then lower to medium heat and cook for 5 minutes.
4) Stir in coconut milk and bring to a boil. Remove from heat and serve. Makes 4 servings.

BUTTERNUT SQUASH SOUP[2]

The flavor of this soup depends on a good quality squash – buy it in season, and you're pretty much guaranteed a delicious soup. I like to roast the seeds and sprinkle on top of the soup, but that's not a necessity.

INGREDIENTS

1 medium butternut squash
3 Tbsp Earth Balance
½ onion (chopped)
1 apple (peeled, cored, and chopped)
1 tsp oil (for roasting seeds)
1/8 tsp salt (for roasting seeds)
2 cups vegetable broth
1 cup coconut milk beverage
1 tsp cinnamon
½ tsp nutmeg
Salt and pepper to taste

PREPARATION

1) Preheat oven to 350 degrees.
2) Slice the squash in half lengthwise and bake flat side down for 45 minutes. Scoop out the seeds, wash them, and put them aside; then scoop out the cooked squash and place in a bowl.
3) In a large saucepan, melt Earth Balance over medium heat. Add chopped onion and cook for 2 minutes.
4) Add apple, stir, and cook covered for 10 minutes.
5) Add the squash, stir, and cook covered for another 10 minutes.
6) Cool slightly, then place into food processor and process until smooth.
7) Mix the squash seeds with oil and salt and bake on a cookie sheet at 350 degrees for 20 minutes or until nicely browned (do not allow to burn).
8) Place processed soup back in the pot and add broth, coconut milk, spices, salt, and pepper. Bring to a boil, then lower to medium heat and cook for 15 minutes.
9) Remove from heat and serve with seeds sprinkled on top. Makes 4 servings.

PASTA FAGIOLI[2]

A hearty soup to warm you up on cold, winter days.

INGREDIENTS

4-5 cups water
½ cup uncooked cannellini beans
2 Tbsp oil
1 small onion
2 celery stalks (chopped)
2 carrots (chopped)
1 tsp crushed garlic
2 Tbsp chopped parsley
4 roma tomatoes
3 cups vegetable broth
1 cup gluten free elbow macaroni
Salt and Pepper to taste.

PREPARATION

1) In a saucepan, bring 2 cups of water to a boil. Turn off heat and add the beans; cover and let sit for 1 hour.
2) Cook over low heat for 1 hr 15 minutes, or until water is absorbed.
3) Add oil to a large pot. Chop onion and cook in oil for 2 minutes.
4) Add celery, carrots, garlic, and parsley. Stir and cook for another 5 minutes.
5) Slice the tops off of the tomatoes and place in a food processor; grind until smooth.
6) Add pureed tomatoes, broth, and 1 cup water to the pot. Stir and cook for 30 minutes.
7) Raise to a slight boil and add macaroni; cook for 10 minutes, stirring occasionally.
8) Add beans, salt, and pepper and stir. Allow to cool to room temperature, as the pasta will absorb more liquid and expand. Add 1-2 cups more water for desired thickness, stir, and heat. Makes 4-6 servings.

QUICHE[3]

Real men and women do eat quiche. You can use a variety of different vegetables in the filling.

INGREDIENTS

Crust
Single pie crust recipe (page 71) – may want to reduce sugar

Filling
1-2 Tbsp oil
½ cup chopped red onion
½ cup chopped mushrooms
½ cup chopped red pepper
½ cup chopped zucchini
2 roma tomatoes, sliced
½ cup Daiya cheddar shreds
6 Tbsp ground chia
1 ½ cups water
1 cup coconut milk beverage
½ cup garbanzo bean flour
½ cup arrowroot starch
¼ cup nutritional yeast
¼ tsp xanthan gum
½ tsp salt

PREPARATION

1) Preheat oven to 350 degrees
2) Press the pie crust dough into the bottom and sides of a 9 inch pie dish which has been sprayed with oil. Flute the edges, and bake for 10 minutes
3) Sautee the vegetables (except tomatoes) in oil for about 5 minutes, or until soft.
4) Spread Daiya shreds over the bottom of the pie crust.
5) Layer tomato slices on top of shreds.
6) Mix the chia and water, and let sit for a few minutes until thick.
7) Add remaining ingredients, and whisk together. Stir in sautéed vegetables.
8) Pour into the pie crust, and bake for 45-50 minutes, or until center is not liquidy. Cool slightly, and serve. Serves 4-6.

PIZZA [3]

This is a pretty basic veggie pizza, but you can experiment with other toppings and sauces. This is a small pizza to serve one to two people.

INGREDIENTS

Dough
½ cup water
1 tsp sugar
1 packet active dry yeast
½ cup brown rice flour
½ cup millet flour
½ cup tapioca flour (plus extra for finishing)
¼ tsp xanthan gum
1/8 tsp salt
1 tsp dried rosemary (optional)
1 Tbsp oil
1 tsp apple cider vinegar

Sauce
1 lb roma tomatoes
¼ cup finely chopped onion
1 tsp crushed garlic
½ tsp oregano
1/8 tsp salt

Topping
1 cup chopped vegetables
1 tsp oil
1/3 cup Daiya mozzarella shreds

PREPARATION

1) To make the dough, heat the water and sugar in a saucepan to between 105 and 115 degrees. Stir until sugar is dissolved.
2) Sprinkle yeast on top of water, and shake pan until yeast is covered with the water. Let set for 15 minutes.
3) Meanwhile, combine remaining dry ingredients in a bowl. Add oil and vinegar and mix well.
4) Make a well in the center, and add the yeast mixture. Stir vigorously to form a soft dough. Work in extra tapioca flour until you can handle the dough without it sticking to your hands.
5) Knead the dough in your hands until smooth and stretchy. Place in a clean bowl and cover with plastic wrap. Let sit for about one hour, until doubled in size.
6) While dough is rising, make the sauce. Core and roughly chop the tomatoes. Place in a food processor and grind until a smooth puree.
7) Place tomato puree and remaining ingredients in a saucepan. Stir and cook until sauce is thick – about 45 minutes.
8) Place a piece of parchment paper on a flat surface. Press risen dough onto center of paper, then flatten it with your hands to a 9 inch circle (use extra starch if dough is too sticky). Shape so there is a thick edge around the outside (this will be the crust). Cover with a large inverted bowl and let rise for another 30 minutes.
9) Preheat oven to 500 degrees with a pizza stone inside (use a cookie sheet if you don't have a pizza stone).
10) For the topping, place oil in a skillet and sautee the vegetables for 3-5 minutes.
11) Once dough has risen, spread the sauce over the top.
12) Sprinkle Daiya shreds evenly on top of the sauce.
13) Cover the shreds with the sautéed vegetables.
14) Lift paper with the pizza and place on top of the stone in the oven. Bake for 10 minutes.
15) Remove pizza and slice.

VEGANAISE[2]

This is seriously the best veganaise I have ever tasted. I think it tastes even better than real mayonnaise.

INGREDIENTS

3 Tbsp thick aquafaba
¼ tsp xanthan gum
1 tsp apple cider vinegar
¼ tsp mustard powder
¼ tsp coconut nectar
1/8 tsp salt
1 cup oil

PREPARATION

1) To get thick aquafaba, take the raw aquafaba (liquid from a can of chickpeas) and cook it down to about ½ cup.
2) In a bowl, blend 3 Tbsp of the aquafaba and xanthan gum with an electric mixer on high speed until a very thick white paste is formed.
3) Add remaining ingredients except oil. Continue mixing at high speed until combined.
4) Add the oil a little at a time while continuing to mix at high speed. Veganaise is done when the texture is smooth and thick. Makes about 1 cup.

SESAME DRESSING[1]

This is my favorite salad dressing; a little bit of sweetness goes a long way.

INGREDIENTS

¾ cup tahini
1 cup oil
¼ cup vinegar (or lemon juice)
3 Tbsp brown rice syrup
4 tsp crushed garlic
1 tsp paprika
¼ tsp salt
¼ tsp pepper

PREPARATION

Combine all ingredients until smooth. Makes about 2 cups.

BUTTERNUT SQUASH[1]

This has just a hint of pumpkin pie. If the squash isn't particularly tasty or sweet, add a little sugar to bring out the flavor.

INGREDIENTS

1 medium butternut squash
1/3 cup chopped parsley
½ tsp cinnamon
1/8 tsp ginger
1/8 tsp nutmeg
Pinch clove

PREPARATION

1) Peel the squash up to the orange interior (through 2 layers – the brown skin and the yellowish white inner skin).
2) Slice off the ends of the squash. Cut into two pieces – the long neck, and the fatter base. Cut the base in half in the opposite direction to expose the seeds. Cut out the center seed sections from each half, and scrape off any remaining seeds.
3) Cut the squash into approximately ½ inch cubes. Place in a steamer pot, and steam for 15-20 minutes or until the desired softness.
4) Mix cooked squash with remaining ingredients and serve. Makes 8-10 servings.

MIXED GREENS[1]

You can use any combination of greens – simply adjust steaming time accordingly.

INGREDIENTS

1 bunch spinach
1 bunch chard
1 bunch kale
1 Tbsp Earth Balance
1 medium onion (finely chopped)
1 Tbsp crushed garlic
1/8 tsp salt
¼ cup pine nuts
3 Tbsp balsamic vinegar

PREPARATION

1) Steam the greens until soft (about 30 minutes for the kale and chard, 10 minutes for the spinach). Press excessive liquid out of the cooked greens.
2) In a large skillet, melt the Earth Balance over medium heat. Add the onion and sautee for 2-3 minutes.
3) Add the garlic and salt, and sautee for another 2-3 minutes.
4) Mix in pine nuts. Spread mixture evenly over pan and continue cooking for 2 more minutes.
5) Lay the greens evenly on top of the onion mixture. Pour the vinegar on top and cook for 2-3 minutes.
6) Mix everything together and continue cooking until greens are desired softness (about 5 more minutes). Makes 6-8 servings.

JAPANESE SWEET POTATOES[2]

This is one of my favorite side dishes. You can use regular potatoes, but the subtle sweetness of Japanese sweet potatoes takes it to the next level.

INGREDIENTS

1 large Japanese sweet potato
1 medium onion (coarsely chopped)
2 Tbsp oil
Salt and pepper to taste
1 tsp paprika

PREPARATION

1) Peel the potato, and cut it into bite sized pieces. Steam for 10 minutes.
2) Heat the oil in a large skillet, and add the chopped onion. Sautee for around 5 minutes, until onions are soft. Add salt and pepper.
3) Add the potatoes, and cook until they are desired softness. Sprinkle on paprika, and cook for another minute. Serve.

BOKCHOY[2]

The bitterness of this vegetable is a nice contrast when you have sweet foods to go with it. I will sometimes add a touch of coconut nectar if the bokchoy is too bitter.

INGREDIENTS

2 bunches of bokchoy
2 Tbsp rice vinegar
3 Tbsp coconut aminos
1 tsp mustard powder
½ tsp ginger

PREPARATION

1) Wash the bokchoy stalks individually, and chop the white stalks like celery stalks. Slice the larger leaves in half; separate the chopped stalks from the leaves.
2) Add the vinegar to a large skillet, and heat it over medium heat.
3) Add the chopped stalks to the skillet, and lay the leaves on top. Cover the pan and cook for 5 minutes.
4) Remove the lid, and add the remaining ingredients. Mix well, and continue cooking until leaves are wilted and soft (5-10 minutes). Serves 6-8.

SQUASH AND MUSHROOMS[1]

This makes a great side dish with a Southwest influence.

INGREDIENTS

1 zucchini squash
1 yellow squash
8 oz mushrooms
2 Tbsp oil
3 Tbsp coconut aminos
2 tsp paprika
½ tsp oregano

PREPARATION

1) Slice the squashes into thick slices; cut in half to make thick semi-circles
2) Quarter the mushrooms
3) Heat the oil in a large skillet. Add the vegetables, and sauté over medium heat for a few minutes, until the mushrooms just start to brown.
4) Add the remaining ingredients, and mix well. Cover the pan, and continue cooking for 5-10 minutes, until the squash is slightly soft.
5) Uncover and continue cooking until the liquid mostly cooks off (you will be left with a thick sauce). Makes 6-8 servings.

NUTTY RICE[2]

If plain rice seems a bit boring, this is a way to turn it up a notch. Makes a great base for a stir fry.

INGREDIENTS

2 cups uncooked brown rice
3 ½ cups water
6 Tbsp coconut aminos
1 cup cashew nuts

PREPARATION

1) Add the rice and water to a medium saucepan. Bring to a boil, then turn heat down to low.
2) Cover with a tight fitting lid, or a lid with something on top to weigh it down (making it as air tight as possible).
3) Continue cooking for 45 minutes.
4) Remove from heat, and let sit for 10 minutes. Remove lid and fluff rice.
5) Add coconut aminos, and mix well.
6) Place nuts in a food processor, and grind to a meal. Add to rice and mix well. Serves 6-8.

MIXED VEGETABLES[2]

The flavors here are subtle, but your mix of veggies will be a hit. You can substitute different vegetables – adjust steam times accordingly.

INGREDIENTS

1 8 oz. package tempeh
1 Tbsp oil
4 Tbsp coconut aminos
2-3 medium carrots sliced
2 cups chopped broccoli
2 cups chopped cauliflower
2 cups sliced mushrooms
1 red pepper chopped
2 Tbsp tahini
1 Tbsp miso paste
1 Tbsp rice vinegar
1 tsp grated ginger
1 tsp paprika

PREPARATION

1) Slice tempeh into ½ inch cubes.
2) In a large skillet, heat oil over medium heat. Sauté tempeh in oil until golden.
3) Add 3 Tbsp coconut aminos and continue sautéing until tempeh is browned. Remove from heat.
4) Steam vegetables until soft: 15 minutes for the carrots, broccoli, and cauliflower, 10 minutes for the red pepper, and 5 minutes for the mushrooms.
5) In a large bowl, combine the remaining 1 Tbsp coconut aminos and remaining ingredients to form a paste.
6) Add tempeh and toss with the paste. Add steamed vegetables and toss together until vegetables are evenly coated. Serves 6-8.

CURRIED LENTILS[1]

This side dish is really easy to make and delicious – you just need a few ingredients. The amount of water and cook time is specific to green lentils, but other types of lentils can be used if those things are adjusted accordingly.

INGREDIENTS

1 cup green lentils
3 cups water
1 Tbsp umeboshi paste
2 tsp curry powder
½ cup chopped green onions

PREPARATION

1) Wash lentils. Place in a large pot with water.
2) Cover with the lid tilted (leaving a space for steam to escape). Cook over medium heat for 20 minutes.
3) Add remaining ingredients, and mix well. Lower heat slightly, and continue cooking for another 5-10 minutes or to desired softness.

GARBANZO BEANS[1]

An Indian influence on the spices make these beans exotic and tasty. For an even simpler version, use canned beans and save the liquid from the can (aquafaba) for a variety of other recipes.

INGREDIENTS

1 cup uncooked garbanzo beans (or 2 15 oz cans of cooked beans)
6 cups water
½ tsp salt
1 tsp cumin
1 tsp paprika
¼ tsp turmeric
½ cup chopped green onions
2 Tbsp lemon juice (or lime juice)

PREPARATION

1) For uncooked beans, rinse the beans, and place in a pot with 3 cups water. Boil for 2 minutes, remove from heat, cover, and let sit for 1 ½ hours. Alternatively, you can just soak beans overnight.
2) Drain beans, and add 6 cups fresh water. Cook over medium heat for 2 hours and 15 minutes (only a little liquid should be left).
3) If using canned beans, drain the liquid (and save it for other recipes!), add 1 cup water, and cook for 10-15 minutes.
4) Add spices and onions, stir, and continue cooking until remaining water is mostly absorbed (about 10 minutes).
5) Add lemon or lime juice and stir. Makes 8-10 servings.

BRUSSEL SPROUTS with COCONUT BACON[3]

A nice mix of salty and sweet. The vinegar gets a little sweet when it's cooked down, but you may also want to sweeten it more with a little coconut nectar.

INGREDIENTS

2 lbs brussel sprouts
¼ cup balsamic vinegar
1 tsp coconut nectar (optional)
1/3 cup coconut flakes
½ tsp oil
1/8 tsp salt

PREPARATION

1) Wash the sprouts, and steam them for 20 minutes. Let them cool until they are no longer too hot to handle.
2) Cut off the ends of the sprouts, and slice them in half lengthwise.
3) Preheat oven to 350 degrees.
4) In a large skillet, heat the vinegar over medium heat. Cook until syrupy.
5) Add the sprouts to the skillet, and mix them to coat with the vinegar. Continue to cook for about 10 minutes turning occasionally, or until the sprouts are browned. If desired, add coconut nectar to add extra sweetness.
6) Mix the coconut flakes with the oil and salt. Spread out on a baking sheet covered with parchment paper.
7) Bake for about 10 minutes, or until flakes are brown and crunchy.
8) Sprinkle coconut flakes over sprouts and serve. Serves 8-10.

CRANBERRY SAUCE[1]

Enjoy this side dish even when it's not Thanksgiving or Christmas. I use honey, which may not be acceptable to some vegans – you can substitute agave and cook it a little longer before adding the cranberries. You can substitute oranges for the tangerines, but the tartness of the tangerines makes this recipe really stand out.

INGREDIENTS

1 cup tangerine juice
1/3 cup honey
Rind of 2 tangerines, thinly sliced
1 12 oz bag cranberries

PREPARATION

1) Place tangerine juice and honey in a medium saucepan. Bring to a boil. Lower to medium heat and cook for around 10 minutes.
2) Wash the cranberries, then add to the saucepan. Stir.
3) Add rind slices and stir.
4) Continue cooking until cranberries have popped and sauce is a little thick, stirring occasionally.
5) Cool and serve.

STUFFING[1]

No one will be able to tell this is gluten-free (as long as you start with a good gluten-free bread). I recommend using the bread recipe from this book – even if it doesn't come out perfectly, it will still be great for stuffing.

INGREDIENTS

2 Tbsp Earth Balance
1 onion, finely chopped
3 celery stalks, sliced
2 tsp crushed or chopped garlic
5 cups gluten-free bread, cut into small cubes
½ cup medjool dates, chopped
2 Tbsp sage
½ tsp coriander
½ tsp salt
¼ tsp pepper
2 ½ cups vegetable broth

PREPARATION

1) Preheat oven to 375 degrees.
2) Melt Earth Balance in a large skillet.
3) Add onion, celery, and garlic, and sauté for around 10 minutes.
4) In a large bowl, combine ingredients from skillet with all remaining ingredients except for ½ cup broth.
5) Pour into an 8X8 inch baking dish and spread evenly. Cover with aluminum foil and bake for 25 minutes.
6) Remove foil, pour remaining broth over top of stuffing, and bake for another 20 minutes uncovered.
7) Cool for 10 minutes and serve. Serves 6-8.

MUSHROOM GRAVY[2]

This gravy can go on a lot of things other than meat – vegetables, mashed potatoes, or stuffing all taste better with gravy on top.

INGREDIENTS

¼ cup Earth Balance
1 cup chopped mushrooms
½ cup chopped onion
2 tsp chopped or crushed garlic
2 cups vegetable broth
¼ tsp black pepper
2 Tbsp arrowroot starch
Coconut milk beverage (optional)

PREPARATION

1) In a skillet, melt Earth Balance.
2) Add mushrooms, onion, and garlic, and sauté for 15-20 minutes.
3) Pour into a food processor along with broth and pepper. Grind until smooth.
4) Pour contents into a saucepan, and bring to a boil. Lower heat and whisk in arrowroot starch. Continue cooking and stirring until thick. If gravy gets too thick, thin it out with a little coconut milk beverage.

KUGEL[2]

This is a tasty version of the traditional side dish. The noodles can be any of a variety of gluten-free options - it will be difficult to find noodles similar to the wide egg noodles used in traditional kugel.

INGREDIENTS

1 cup cashews (plus water for soaking)
1 ¼ cups water
3 Tbsp ground chia seeds
1 can coconut milk (chilled for a few days)
¼ cup sugar
¼ cup Earth Balance
1 Tbsp apple cider vinegar
1 Tbsp lemon juice
1 Tbsp nutritional yeast
8 oz gluten free pasta (rigatoni, penne, or other similar noodles)
4 Tbsp agar agar flakes
¼ cup raisins
Cinnamon for topping

PREPARATION

1) Soak cashews in water for several hours.
2) Drain cashews and place in a food processor with ½ cup water. Grind until smooth. Pour into a large saucepan.
3) Preheat oven to 375 degrees.
4) In a small bowl, combine chia and ¾ cup water. Let sit for 5 minutes until thick. Add to cashew mixture.
5) Open coconut milk, and scoop out thick cream that has risen to the top. Add to the saucepan.
6) Add sugar, Earth Balance, vinegar, and nutritional yeast. Heat to melt and combine ingredients.
7) Meanwhile, bring a large pot of water to a boil. Add pasta, and cook for 5 minutes, stirring occasionally. Remove from heat.
8) Bring cashew mixture to a boil. Lower heat, and whisk in agar agar. Continue cooking for 3-5 more minutes, stirring occasionally. Remove from heat.
9) Drain and rinse pasta. Add to cashew mixture along with raisins, and stir together.
10) Spray an 8X8 inch baking dish with oil, and pour the pasta mixture into the dish. Spread evenly, and sprinkle top with cinnamon. Bake for 45 minutes, or until nicely browned on top.
11) Allow to cool and set for at least one hour. Heat up when ready to serve. Serves 6-8.

BROCCOLI PESTO PENNE[2]

An alternative to traditional pesto- also a great way to use up some extra broccoli.

INGREDIENTS

1 ½ cups broccoli (coarsely chopped)
¾ cup walnuts
¼ cup Daiya mozzarella cheese shreds
2 tsp crushed garlic
3 Tbsp oil
6 Tbsp Earth Balance
1 medium onion (finely chopped)
1 red pepper (chopped)
1 cup coconut milk beverage
Salt and pepper to taste
3 cups gluten-free penne

PREPARATION

1) In a food processor, combine the broccoli, walnuts, cheese, garlic, and oil. Grind until smooth.
2) In a large saucepan, melt the Earth Balance over medium heat and add the chopped onion. Sauté for about 2 minutes then add the chopped pepper; cook for another 2 minutes.
3) Add the ground pesto and coconut milk, salt and pepper, mix, and cook over low heat for about 10 minutes.
4) Cook the pasta according to package directions, drain, and toss with the pesto sauce. Serves 4;

SWEET POTATO GNOCCHI[3]

Regular potatoes can be used, but sweet potatoes add a nice extra flavor. I recommend Hannah sweet potatoes or another variety with light colored insides; the orange varieties tend to be too watery - they can work, but need to be dried out first before grinding. This recipe uses a creamy pesto sauce, but you can use any sauce of your choosing.

INGREDIENTS

Gnocchi
1 lb sweet potatoes (avoid varieties with orange
        insides – too much liquid)
1 cup tapioca flour

Sauce
2 cups packed basil
1/3 cup pine nuts
½ cup Daiya mozzarella shreds
1/3 cup oil
3 tsp crushed garlic
½ tsp salt
½ medium onion
¼ cup Earth Balance
1 cup coconut milk beverage
Chopped parsley for topping

PREPARATION

1) Fill a large pot with water; bring to a boil, and boil the potatoes for 45 minutes.
2) Once potatoes have cooled, peel them and place them into a food processor; grind until completely smooth.
3) Mix with tapioca flour to create a soft dough. Add more starch if too sticky. Chill for 30 minutes.
4) Break off a 2-3 inch ball of dough, and roll on a sheet of wax paper with your hands to form a long snake (about ½ inch in diameter).
5) With a sharp knife, slice the snake into 1 inch long pieces; set aside on a plate or another piece of wax paper.
6) Continue to roll out and slice the rest of the dough in the same manner. Gnocchi can also be frozen to cook at a later time.
7) Make the sauce by first placing the basil, pine nuts, Daiya, oil, garlic, and salt into a food processor. Grind until smooth.
8) Finely chop onion. Melt Earth Balance in a large saucepan over medium heat, and add the onion. Continue to cook until transparent (5-10 minutes). Be sure to stir the onions frequently so they don't burn.
9) Add pesto and coconut milk beverage, and continue cooking until thick.
10) To cook the gnocchi, bring a large pot of water to a boil; add gnocchi and boil for about 3 minutes. Drain, and add to the pesto sauce. Cook together for a minute or two. Sprinkle chopped parsley on top. Serves 4.

RAVIOLI[5]

This dish can be a bit time consuming, and it takes some practice to get it just right – you want the dough to be thin, but you don't want it to tear or open up. Gluten free doughs are very delicate, so be gentle.

INGREDIENTS

Filling
1 cup cashew nuts (plus water for soaking)
¼ cup water
1 Tbsp nutritional yeast
1 Tbsp white miso paste
2 cloves garlic
½ tsp chopped parsley

Shells
1 cup brown rice flour
1 cup tapioca flour (+ extra for rolling out)
½ tsp xanthan gum
2/3 cup boiling water
1/3 cup cold water

Sauce
¼ cup Earth Balance
1 onion (finely chopped)
4 cups chopped mushrooms
4 cups coconut milk beverage
1 1/3 cups Daiya mozzarella shreds

PREPARATION

1) For the filling, soak the cashew nuts in water for a couple of hours. Drain and place in a food processor with remaining ingredients. Blend until smooth.

2) For the sauce, melt the Earth Balance in a saucepan over medium heat. Add onions and cook until golden, stirring often (about 10 minutes). Add mushrooms, stir, and cook for 2-3 minutes. Add coconut milk beverage and cook for another 5 minutes. Add shreds, and cook until smooth and thick.

3) To make the shells, combine the dry ingredients in a bowl. Make a well in the center, and add the boiling water. Stir vigorously. Add cold water and continue stirring until a soft dough forms – add more starch if too sticky.

4) Flour a piece of wax paper with a little tapioca flour. Cover half the dough in flour, and press onto the paper. Place another piece of wax paper on top, and roll out to a about 1/16 inch in thickness. Periodically remove the top paper and add extra flour if it is getting too sticky.

5) Using a glass or cookie cutter, cut out 2 ½ inch circles of dough. Place a teaspoon of filling in the center, then fold in half and press the edges together (wet the edges first if it's too dry). Set filled shells aside on another piece of wax paper. Gather up unused dough to be rolled out again.

6) Continue the rolling out process until all dough is used. Bring a large pot of water to a boil, and add the shells to the boiling water (don't cook too many shells at one time). Lower heat a little, and cook shells for 7-8 minutes. Remove with a slotted spoon, and serve with sauce. Makes about 4 dozen ravioli.

MACARONI AND CHEESE[2]

An all American comfort food. Traditionalists may not like the addition of broccoli, but I think it makes this version stand out.

INGREDIENTS

2 cups gluten free macaroni
¼ cup Earth Balance
1 cup finely chopped onion
2 tsp crushed garlic
½ tsp salt
2 cups chopped broccoli
1 tsp chopped parsley
1 tsp chopped basil
3 cups coconut milk beverage
1 ½ cups Daiya cheddar cheese shreds
½ cup Daiya Mozzarella cheese shreds
½ cup gluten free bread crumbs

PREPARATION

1) Preheat oven to 350 degrees.
2) Fill a large pot with water and bring to a boil. Add macaroni and cook for a few minutes shorter than the package directions. Drain and set aside.
3) In a large saucepan, melt Earth Balance and add chopped onion. Cover and cook over medium heat, stirring occasionally, until golden.
4) Stir in crushed garlic and salt. Cook until garlic browns.
5) Stir in broccoli and cook for a few minutes.
6) Add coconut milk beverage, parsley, and basil, and bring to a boil.
7) Add cheese shreds, and cook over medium heat until smooth.
8) Add cooked macaroni and mix well.
9) Pour into an 8 X 8 inch baking dish, and sprinkle bread crumbs evenly on top.
10) Bake for 30 minutes. Cool for 10 minutes and serve. Serves 4-6.

POTSTICKERS[4]

These make a great appetizer. You can experiment with different fillings – just chop everything finely. This is very similar to making ravioli, though you can get away with thicker dough (not quite as delicate).

INGREDIENTS

Hoisin Sauce
2 Tbsp peanut butter
2 Tbsp coconut aminos
2 tsp rice vinegar
2 tsp sesame oil
1 tsp coconut nectar
1 tsp chopped garlic
1/8 tsp black pepper

Filling
1 cup finely shredded cabbage
¼ tsp salt
1 cup Beyond Beef crumbles (defrosted)
1 cup shiitake mushrooms (finely chopped)
2 Tbsp green onion (finely chopped)
1 Tbsp Hoisin Sauce
1 tsp grated ginger
½ tsp coconut aminos
½ tsp rice vinegar
½ tsp sesame oil

Wraps
1 cup brown rice flour
1 cup tapioca flour (plus extra for rolling out)
½ tsp xanthan gum
2/3 cup boiling water
1/3 cup cold water

PREPARATION

1) Make the sauce first, since you will need some for the filling. Mix all ingredients until well combined.
2) Next, make the filling. Combine cabbage and salt, and let sit for 10 minutes (the salt will draw the liquid from the cabbage).
3) Squeeze out and discard the excess liquid from the cabbage. Combine with remaining ingredients, and set aside.
4) To make the dough for the wraps, combine the dry ingredients. Add boiling water and stir with a fork until well combined and crumbly.
5) Add cold water a little at a time until dough is soft and sticky. Stir vigorously until dough gets a little stretchy.
6) Work in a little more tapioca flour with your hands until dough is smooth and not sticky.
7) Flour a piece of wax paper with some tapioca flour. Take half the dough, and cover it with flour. Press it onto the paper, and place another piece of wax paper on top. Roll out to between 1/8 and 1/16 inch, frequently removing the top paper to add more flour if it gets too sticky.
8) Using a large glass or cookie cutter, cut dough into 3 inch circles; gather up unused dough to be rolled out again later.
9) Loosen the circles of dough using a spatula. Wet the outside edges with your finger. Place a circle in the palm of your hand, and spoon a tablespoon of filling onto the center of the circle. Bring the centers together and pinch together. Pinch together the corners. Pinch together halfway between each corner and the center. Continue this way to finish off the rest of the openings. Set aside, and repeat with remaining circles.
10) Continue rolling out remaining dough, and fill and close the potstickers until all dough is used.
11) To cook the potstickers, heat a large skillet (which has a lid) over medium heat. Have ¼ cup of water ready, and have the lid nearby.
12) Once the skillet is hot, add a little oil and swirl it around to coat the bottom. Arrange half the potstickers in the skillet, and cook them until the bottoms just start to brown. If the skillet does not have a non-stick surface, frequently loosen the bottoms with a spatula to keep them from sticking.
13) Holding the lid in one hand, and the water in the other, pour the water into the skillet; immediately cover with the lid (this will steam the potstickers). Let them steam this way for about 3 minutes.
14) Remove the lid, and continue cooking until the bottoms are nicely browned. As each potsticker browns, remove from the skillet and place on a paper towel to drain. Cook the remaining potstickers the same way.
15) Serve with the Hoisin sauce for dipping. Makes 3 dozen.

PIEROGIES[4]

This is a traditional Polish dish with a lot of variations. It's yet another form of "ravioli."

INGREDIENTS

Sour Cream
1 can coconut milk
        (left in refrigerator for several days)
1 Tbsp apple cider vinegar

Filling
¾ lbs russet potatoes (1 medium potato)
2 Tbsp Earth Balance
2 tsp crushed garlic
¼ tsp salt
¼ cup coconut milk beverage
¼ cup Daiya cheddar shreds

Dough
1 Tbsp ground chia seeds
¼ cup water
¼ cup Earth Balance (plus extra for browning)
½ cup vegan sour cream
2/3 cups brown rice flour
2/3 cups millet flour
2/3 cups tapioca flour + extra for rolling out
½ tsp xanthan gum

PREPARATION

1) For the filling, boil the potatoes for 45 minutes. Mash and combine with remaining ingredients, cooking over low heat until smooth.

2) For the sour cream, scoop out the thick cream from the top of the coconut milk. Mix with vinegar until smooth.

3) For the dough, combine chia and water. Let sit for a few minutes until thick.

4) Cream Earth Balance with the chia mixture. Add remaining ingredients and beat vigorously until a dough is formed; add extra tapioca flour if too sticky.

5) Flour a piece of wax paper with tapioca flour. Take half the dough, and cover it with flour. Press flat onto the wax paper, and add extra flour to the top. Cover with another piece of wax paper, and roll out to 1/16 inch thickness. Periodically remove top paper and add more flour if dough gets sticky.

6) Using a small glass or cookie cutter, cut out 2 ½ inch circles from the dough. Save scraps to be rolled out again.

7) Wet the edges of the circles. Place 1 tsp filling in the centers, and fold in half. Press edges together with a fork, and set aside (on another piece of wax paper). Continue rolling out until all dough used.

8) Bring a large pot of water to a boil. Add shells and boil for 5 minutes (don't cook too many at one time).

9) If desired, brown shells in a little Earth Balance on both sides. Makes around 3 dozen.

QUINOA RISOTTO[3]

One of my all time favorite meals. I had this in a restaurant in North Carolina, and immediately set out to try to duplicate it.

INGREDIENTS

Balsamic Reduction
1 cup balsamic vinegar
½ tsp coconut nectar

Cashew Cream
1 cup cashew nuts
     (soaked in water for several hours)
1 cup coconut milk beverage

Risotto
¼ cup earth balance
½ medium onion (finely chopped)
2 tsp crushed garlic
1 cup quinoa
2 cups water
4 cups coconut milk beverage
Salt and pepper to taste

Vegetable Topping
1 bunch chard
1 small yellow squash (sliced about 1/8 inch thick)
8-10 mushrooms (sliced in half)

PREPARATION

1) Make the balsamic reduction first. Cook vinegar in a saucepan until reduced and coats the pan; do not let it burn.
2) Cool vinegar and stir in coconut nectar. Pour into a squeeze bottle.
3) For the coconut cream, drain the nuts and blend in a food processor with coconut milk until smooth.
4) In a large pot, melt Earth Balance and add chopped onion. Continue cooking until onions turn golden – stir occasionally to prevent burning.
5) Add garlic and continue cooking for another 2-3 minutes.
6) Add quinoa, water, salt and pepper. Cook over medium heat until water is absorbed, stirring occasionally.
7) Steam chard until soft (about 20 minutes)
8) Add coconut milk to quinoa one cup at a time, allowing each addition to get absorbed by the quinoa.
9) Add coconut cream and mix well. Cook until a good creamy consistence.
10) Sautee squash and mushrooms in a little oil until soft.
11) To serve, place a helping of risotto on a plate. Arrange squash and mushrooms on top. Drizzle balsamic reduction over that. Lay leaves of chard on, and drizzle more balsamic reduction generously on top.

STUFFED CABBAGE[3]

I use quinoa for this stuffing, but you can always use the more traditional rice in its place. I really wanted to make these with red cabbage – it's doable, but the leaves are much tougher and it just doesn't work as well as green cabbage.

INGREDIENTS

1 head green cabbage
6 roma tomatoes (1 ½ lbs)
½ cup uncooked quinoa
2 cups water
¼ cup Earth Balance
1 sweet onion (finely chopped)
2 cups chopped mushrooms
1 bag Beyond Meat crumbles
1 tsp paprika
½ tsp salt
6 medjool dates (pitted)

PREPARATION

1) Bring a large pot of water to a boil. Remove the core of the cabbage, and place core side down into the pot. Boil for 10-15 minutes.
2) Using 2 forks, turn the cabbage over and continue cooking. As the outer leaves start to separate, carefully pull them off using the forks, and place them into a bowl to cool. Once you have removed 12-13 leaves, turn the heat down, and let the remaining cabbage continue cooking slowly for another 10-20 minutes. Remove the remaining leaves and set aside.
3) Remove the tops of the tomatoes, coarsely chop, and place into a food processor. Blend until smooth. Pour into a saucepan and cook over medium heat until the consistency of pasta sauce (about 45 minutes).
4) Combine the quinoa and water in a saucepan, and cook over medium heat until the water is absorbed (15-20 minutes).
5) In a large skillet, melt Earth Balance over medium heat. Add chopped onion, and cook until golden brown (stirring frequently).
6) Add chopped mushrooms to the onions, and continue cooking until mushrooms are soft.
7) Mix in crumbles, and cook until fully heated. Mix in paprika and salt.
8) Chop dates, and mix into beef mixture. Cook for a few minutes more. Combine with quinoa and tomato sauce.
9) Preheat oven to 350 degrees.
10) One by one, take a cabbage leaf, and, using a sharp knife, slice through the thick stem to remove it's thickness. Place the meat filling on the inside of the leaf, toward the stem. Roll around the filling once, then fold in the sides. Continue rolling to the end of the leaf. Place seam side down in a 9X13 baking dish.
11) Continue rolling leaves until the dish is packed full. Place any leftover leaves on top of the rolls. Cover dish with foil, and bake for 1 ½ hours. Remove leaves from the tops of the rolls and serve. Makes 12-14 rolls.

LASAGNA[3]

This is another big favorite of mine – you may think you're eating real meat lasagna!

INGREDIENTS

Sauce
3 lbs roma tomatoes
1 onion
4 tsp crushed garlic
1 tsp oregano
1 tsp salt
¼ tsp pepper
1 package Beyond Meat crumbles

Cheese
2 cups cashew nuts (soaked in water for several hours)
½ cup water
1 Tbsp nutritional yeast
2 Tbsp white miso paste
3 cloves garlic
1 tsp chopped parsley

Noodles
1 pkg gluten free lasagna noodles

Topping
½ cup Daiya mozzarella shreds

PREPARATION

1) Slice off tops of tomatoes, coarsely chop, and place in food processor. Grind until smooth.
2) Place tomato puree into a large pot. Finely chop onion (or pulse in food processor) and add to tomatoes. Add spices, stir, and bring to a boil; lower heat and cook until thick (about 45 minutes)
3) Add beef crumbles to sauce, and continue cooking until extra water is gone.
4) Bring a large pot of water to a boil; add lasagna noodles, and cook until soft. Drain, and lay noodles on paper towels to dry.
5) Make cheese by draining soaked nuts and combining with all other ingredients in a food processor; grind until smooth and creamy.
6) Preheat oven to 350 degrees
7) Assemble lasagna by spooning sauce onto bottom of an 8 X 8 inch baking dish. Lay noodles across bottom to cover sauce (can overlap slightly). If some noodles are broken, use those on the bottom layers, saving whole noodles for the top. Tear off excess length of noodles if they are longer than the pan.
8) Spoon more sauce on top of noodles. Spread half of the cheese on top of the sauce. Cover with more noodles, laid in the opposite direction of the bottom layer.
9) Continue layering with sauce, cheese, and noodles. Cover top noodles with remaining sauce. Sprinkle Daiya cheese on top of sauce.
10) Bake uncovered for 50-55 minutes. Let cool for 15 minutes before serving. Serves 6-8.

JACKFRUIT STEW[2]

This makes a hearty, filling stew. Serve it over rice or quinoa.

INGREDIENTS

1 medium onion, finely chopped
2 Tbsp oil
2 tsp crushed garlic
1 ½ lbs roma tomatoes
4 cups vegetable broth
¼ cup coconut aminos
1 tsp cumin
1 tsp coriander
1 tsp paprika
2 lbs potatoes, chopped
2 large carrots, sliced
2 celery stalks, sliced
1 20 oz. can jackfruit
2 Tbsp arrowroot starch

PREPARATION

1) In a large skillet, sautee the onion in the oil over medium heat until tender. Add garlic and sautee for a couple more minutes.
2) Slice the tops off the tomatoes, and place in a food processor. Process until a smooth puree.
3) Add tomato puree and 2 cups broth to the onions, along with the coconut aminos and spices. Stir.
4) Mix in vegetables, and cook for 20 minutes; stir occasionally so that nothing burns.
5) Wash and drain jackfruit. Add to skillet with 1 cup broth. Stir and cook for 20 minutes.
6) Combine remaining broth with the arrowroot starch, and add to the skillet. Stir together until well combined. Cook for another 15 minutes, or until potatoes are soft. Stir frequently to prevent burning. Serve over rice or quinoa. Makes 8-10 servings.

FOOD COLORING[1]

I always prefer to use natural food coloring when possible. The entire rainbow is achievable, using fruits and vegetables. Here are examples of an assortment of colors to achieve from natural ingredients. Their flavors can easily be covered with other ingredients (like sugar), unless you actually want the flavors to come through.

RED:

Pureed beets – peel and puree beets and add directly to your food. You can also thinly slice the beets, dry them in a low heat oven, and grind them into a powder.

Alternatives: raspberries, cherries (pureed or dried)

ORANGE:

Pureed carrots – peel and puree carrots and add directly to your food.

Alternatives: oranges, tangerines (juice, rind)

YELLOW:

Turmeric – a little turmeric goes a long way toward a yellow color. It has a strong flavor, so use sparingly.

Alternatives: lemons, yellow peppers (rind, puree)

GREEN:

Spirulina – you can find this powder in the health food section of your supermarket, or at a vitamin/supplement store.

Alternatives: basil, spinach (pureed)

BLUE, INDIGO, VIOLET

Red Cabbage – this one vegetable offers a whole range of colors. Simply boil the cabbage for 30 minutes to get purple water. Remove the cabbage, and continue boiling the water down to a few tablespoons of deep purple coloring. To get indigo, mix in a touch of baking soda. To get blue, add a bit more. The more baking soda you add, the more it will go towards green.

Alternatives: blueberries

BASIC PIE CRUST[3]

This a basic step for many desserts – not just pies. The dough is very soft, so you can shape it with your hands – you don't need to roll it out.

INGREDIENTS

1/3 cup Earth Balance
3 Tbsp sugar
1/3 cup brown rice flour
1/3 cup millet flour
1/3 cup tapioca flour
¼ tsp xanthan gum
3 Tbsp water

PREPARATION

1) Cream the Earth Balance and sugar until smooth.
2) Separately combine the remaining dry ingredients; add to the Earth Balance mixture, and blend to form a crumbly texture.
3) Add the water, and stir vigorously until a soft dough is formed. Knead the dough for a few seconds. Add more tapioca flour if it's too sticky.
4) If making a pie, press the dough into a pie dish which has been sprayed with oil. Spread the dough with your fingers to cover the bottom and up and over the sides of the dish. Push dough around to cover any holes which are formed.
5) Even out the edges, and flute them. Be sure to especially press the dough into the corner between the sides and bottom, as that area can easily become too thick.
6) If baking the crust, poke holes in the bottom with a fork to allow air to escape. A prebaked crust should bake for 20 minutes in a 375 degree oven.

COCONUT WHIPPED CREAM[2]

I think this tastes even better than dairy whipped cream. It's easy to make, and can be added to a lot of different desserts. I HIGHLY recommend using the Whole Foods brand (365) of coconut milk – I find it separates very quickly, and you can often scoop out the cream without even refrigerating it. However, it's always safer to err on the side of chilling for a longer time; if the cream is too hard, you can always add water, but if it's too watery you're only choice is to put it back in the fridge until it separates.

INGREDIENTS

1 can coconut milk (**NOT** light) left in fridge
    from 1-3 days
1 tsp vanilla extract
3 Tbsp powdered sugar

PREPARATION

1) Open the can of coconut milk, and scoop out the thick cream from the top (it may be pretty hard). Place in a mixing bowl.
2) If the cream is hard, add a little of the liquid left in the can and cream it with a fork until soft and creamy.
3) Beat with an electric mixer until thick and creamy. Add vanilla, and mix some more.
4) Add sugar, and beat for a few minutes to a good consistency.

COCONUT CREAM PIE[3]

I was never a huge fan of this dessert traditionally, but this is now one of my favorites. A must for coconut lovers.

INGREDIENTS

Crust
Single Pie Crust recipe

Filling
1 cup shredded coconut
1 cup brown rice syrup
2 cups almond milk
1 tsp vanilla extract
2 Tbsp agar agar flakes

Topping
Double coconut whipped cream recipe (page 71)

PREPARATION

1) Preheat oven to 375 degrees.
2) Use your hands to press the pie dough evenly over the bottom, up and over the sides of a pie dish which has been sprayed with oil. Prick bottom of crust with a fork, and bake for 20 minutes.
3) Lower oven temperature to 350 degrees.
4) Cover a cookie sheet with parchment paper, and spread shredded coconut over the surface. Bake for 3 minutes, mix shreds, and bake another 2 minutes to toast evenly.
5) For the filling, place ¾ cup of the toasted shreds, rice syrup, almond milk, and vanilla extract into a saucepan; bring to a boil, stirring occasionally.
6) Mix in agar agar flakes, and continue cooking for 5 minutes, stirring occasionally.
7) Place ice cubes into a large bowl, and set saucepan on top - this will quickly cool the mixture. Once mixture gets a little thickened, stir and pour into the baked pie crust.
8) Chill pie until filling sets – an hour or two.
9) Mix up coconut whipped cream, and spoon on top of the filling (or use a pastry bag for a more decorative pie).
10) Sprinkle remaining coconut shreds on top. Keep refrigerated.

PECAN PIE[3]

Pecan pie was always one of my favorite desserts; this version comes pretty close to the real thing.

INGREDIENTS

Crust
Basic Pie Crust (page 71)

Filling
1 cup medjool dates
2 cups water
¾ cup brown rice syrup
¼ cup coconut butter
2 Tbsp agar agar flakes
1 ½ cups pecan halves

PREPARATION

1) Preheat oven to 375 degrees.
2) For crust, press the dough evenly over the bottom, up and over the sides of a pie dish which has been sprayed with oil. Even out the edges and flute the crust. Bake for 15 minutes.
3) Place dates and water into a food processor and grind until smooth.
4) Place date puree, rice syrup, and coconut butter into a medium saucepan; bring to a boil.
5) Lower heat and stir until smooth. Add agar agar and continue stirring until mixture thickens slightly (about 5 minutes)
6) Layer pecans on bottom of baked pie shell. Pour filling over pecans and bake for 10 minutes.
7) Let pie cool, then refrigerate overnight to set.

LEMON MERINGUE PIE[3]

It took a while to figure out the best way to achieve the meringue top. I've looked at several options for baking the aquafaba, and this version seems the best. Plan a couple of days ahead to achieve the best result.

INGREDIENTS

Crust
Single Pie Crust recipe (page 71)

Filling
1/3 cup lemon juice
1 cup agave
¼ cup kuzu
2 ½ cups almond milk
1/8 tsp turmeric
2 Tbsp agar agar flakes

Meringue
Liquid from 1 15 oz can of garbanzo beans
¼ tsp cream of tartar
1 tsp vanilla extract
½ cup powdered sugar

PREPARATION

1) Preheat oven to 375 degrees.
2) Mix up a single pie crust recipe and press the dough into the bottom and sides of a pie dish which has been sprayed with oil. Flute the edges, prick the bottom with a fork and bake for 20 minutes. Cool.
3) Prep the meringue by boiling the garbanzo bean liquid (aquafaba) until it cooks down to ½ cup.
4) To make the filling, place the kuzu in a small bowl and crush it with the back of a fork. Add ¼ cup almond milk, and mix until fully dissolved.
5) Place remaining almond milk and other ingredients except the agar agar in a medium saucepan. Bring to a boil.
6) Lower heat and whisk in the kuzu mixture, then whisk in the agar agar. Continue cooking for 5 more minutes, stirring occasionally.
7) Remove from heat, and allow to cool. Pour into the baked pie shell. Chill over night to completely set.
8) Preheat oven to 400 degrees.
9) For the meringue, beat the aquafaba with the cream of tartar at high speed until peaks form (3-5 minutes). Add vanilla and continue beating until fully combined.
10) Add powdered sugar a little at a time, and continue beating until very stiff peaks form (another 5-10 minutes). Pipe or spoon on top of the pie
11) Bake for 5 minutes or until meringue tips brown. Cool and chill. Pie can be served once cool, though the meringue top may be very sticky (will cut easily with a heated knife). For better results, allow to chill for at least a day before serving, and the meringue should be easy to cut through.

SUGAR PIE[3]

I had never heard of (or tasted) this pie, but a friend from Montreal (where it is very popular) told me about it. It's similar to pecan pie without the pecans, and quite tasty.

INGREDIENTS

Crust
Single Pie Crust recipe (page 71)

Filling
2 Tbsp kuzu
1 cup almond milk
1 can coconut milk
1 cup dark sugar
1/3 cup maple syrup
¼ cup brown rice flour
¼ cup Earth Balance
1 Tbsp agar agar flakes

PREPARATION

1) Preheat oven to 375 degrees.
2) For crust, press the dough evenly over the bottom, up and over the sides of a pie dish. Even out the edges and flute the crust.
3) Bake for 20 minutes. Cool.
4) For the filling, combine kuzu and ¼ cup almond milk in a small bowl until fully dissolved.
5) Place remaining almond milk and all other ingredients except agar agar in a medium saucepan. Bring to a boil.
6) Lower heat, and whisk in kuzu mixture. Whisk in agar agar. Cook for 5 minutes, stirring frequently.
7) Pour filling into baked pie shell. Cool and chill for several hours, or until set.

TANGERINE TART[2]

I love the combination of the tart tangerines with the chocolaty carob (or chocolate) crust.

INGREDIENTS

Crust
Single Pie Crust recipe (page 71)
2 Tbsp unsweetened carob powder
     (can replace with cocoa powder)

Filling
1 lb tangerines
1 ½ cups almond milk
1 cup agave
¼ cup kuzu

PREPARATION

1) Preheat oven to 375 degrees
2) Mix carob powder with basic pie crust dough, and press into the bottom and sides of a tart dish.
3) Bake crust for 20 minutes. Set aside to cool.
4) Peel tangerines and remove seeds (if there are any). Place in a food processor and grind to a smooth puree.
5) Place puree, 1 cup almond milk, and agave into a medium saucepan. Crush kuzu and combine with remaining almond milk until fully dissolved.
6) Stir puree mixture, and bring to a boil. Lower heat, and stir in kuzu mixture. Continue cooking until mixture starts to thicken (5 minutes). Remove from heat and allow to cool.
7) Pour filling into baked crust, and chill for several hours or overnight to set.

BOSTON CREAM PIE[3]

I never understood why this is called pie, when it's really cake; either way, it makes for a delicious dessert.

INGREDIENTS

Cake
4 Tbsp chia seeds
1 cup water
2/3 cup apple sauce
2/3 cup agave
1/4 cup oil
1 tsp apple cider vinegar
1 1/3 cups brown rice flour
2/3 cup tapioca flour
1 ½ tsp baking soda
½ tsp xanthan gum

Filling
1 can coconut milk (left in refrigerator for a few days)
2 tsp vanilla extract
¼ cup agave
1 ½ Tbsp kuzu
½ cup almond milk

Frosting
2 Tbsp coconut butter
1 cup powdered sugar
3 Tbsp carob powder (or cocoa powder)
3 Tbsp almond milk

PREPARATION

1) Preheat oven to 375 degrees
2) In a large mixing bowl, combine chia seeds and water. Let sit for 5 minutes. Stir.
3) Add remaining ingredients and mix well.
4) Divide batter between two 9 inch spring form pans which have been sprayed with oil
5) Bake for 15-20 minutes, or until a toothpick comes out clean.
6) Cool layers slightly, remove from pans, and chill.
7) For filling, scoop out thick cream from coconut milk can and place in a medium saucepan. Add vanilla and agave. Heat until smooth.
8) Place kuzu in a bowl and crush with the back of a fork. Add almond milk and mix until fully dissolved.
9) Bring contents of saucepan to a boil. Lower heat and add kuzu mixture. Continue cooking while whisking for 5 minutes to form a pudding.
10) Let filling cool, then chill until thick. Place one cake layer upside down on a serving dish, top with filling, then place other layer on top right side up.
11) To make frosting, melt coconut butter in a saucepan over low heat. Mix in sugar and carob powder.
12) Add almond milk a little at a time until a frosting is formed which can be poured (but not too thin).
13) While still warm, pour frosting on top of cake and spread to edges (letting it drip down the sides).
14) Chill until frosting is hard.

SQUASH PIE[3]

This tastes just like pumpkin pie; I prefer to use butternut squash, because the flavor and texture tend to be more consistent than pumpkin.

INGREDIENTS

Crust
Single Pie Crust recipe (page 71)

Filling
2 cups butternut squash puree
¾ cup sugar
2 tsp cinnamon
½ tsp nutmeg
½ tsp ginger
1/8 tsp clove
2 cans coconut milk, chilled for several days
¼ cup kuzu

PREPARATION

1) Preheat oven to 375 degrees.
2) For crust, press the dough evenly over the bottom, up and over the sides of a pie dish. Even out the edges and flute the crust.
3) Bake for 20 minutes. Cool.
4) To make the squash puree, slice a medium squash in half lengthwise. Place both halves face down on a baking sheet covered with parchment paper.
5) Bake at 350 degrees for 45 minutes. Let cool, and scoop out the seeds.
6) Scoop out the cooked squash and place into a food processor; grind until smooth.
7) Place puree, sugar, and spices in a large saucepan. Open cans of coconut milk, and scoop out the thick cream from the top – add cream to the saucepan.
8) In a small bowl, crush the kuzu with a fork until powdery. Add a little of the water from the cans of coconut milk and mix well to form a paste.
9) Bring the ingredients in the saucepan to a boil, stirring occasionally.
10) Lower heat and whisk in the kuzu mixture. Continue cooking for another 5 minutes, stirring frequently.
11) Pour filling into baked pie shell. Cool and chill until set.

PUMPKIN BARS[3]

I call these pumpkin bars, but, again, I make them with butternut squash (no one will know the difference).

INGREDIENTS

Crust
5 medjool dates
2 Tbsp coconut butter
1 ½ cups slivered almonds

Cake
1 cup butternut squash puree
2 Tbsp ground white chia seeds
½ cup water
¼ cup Earth Balance
2 tsp vanilla extract
½ cup dark sugar
1 tsp cinnamon
¼ tsp ginger
¼ tsp nutmeg
Pinch clove
1 Tbsp baking powder
1/3 cup brown rice flour
1/3 cup millet flour
1/3 cup arrowroot starch
¼ tsp xanthan gum

Frosting
3 Tbsp coconut butter
1 ¼ cups powdered sugar
3 Tbsp carob powder (can use cocoa powder)
1 tsp vanilla extract
2 Tbsp almond milk

PREPARATION

1) To make the squash puree, slice a butternut squash in half lengthwise; bake in a 350 degree oven face down on a cookie sheet covered in parchment paper for 45 minutes. Let cool, and scoop out and discard the seeds. Scoop out the squash, and puree in a food processor until smooth. Set aside.
2) Preheat the oven to 375 degrees.
3) Make the crust by placing dates and coconut butter in a food processor; blend until smooth. Place contents in a bowl.
4) Finely chop the almonds in a food processor – don't grind them too fine. Mix the almonds with the date mixture until fully blended.
5) Press the crust mixture into the bottom of an 8X8 inch baking dish which has been sprayed with oil and lightly floured with some brown rice flour. Bake for 5 minutes.
6) Mix chia seeds and water in a large bowl, and let sit until a thick paste is formed.
7) Add remaining cake ingredients and mix well. Stir vigorously to activate the xanthan gum.
8) Pour batter on top of the crust, and spread evenly. Bake for about 35 minutes, or until the center is well cooked.
9) Make the frosting by placing all ingredients except almond milk in a saucepan; heat over low heat and stir until coconut butter is melted. Add almond milk and continue stirring until a good spreading consistency.
10) Pour frosting on top of warm cake and spread quickly before it gets too hard. If frosting does harden, run the knife in hot water to make spreading easier.
11) Let cool, chill, and cut into bars. Makes two dozen.

APPLE MANDARIN CAKE[2]

An unusual but great combination of flavors – apple and mandarin orange.

INGREDIENTS

8 small mandarin oranges (about 1 lb)
4 Tbsp ground white chia seeds
¾ cup water
1/3 cup oil
1 tsp apple cider vinegar
½ cup almond milk
1 cup sugar
2/3 cup brown rice flour
2/3 cup millet flour
2/3 cup arrowroot starch
1 Tbsp baking powder
1 tsp baking soda
2 large apples

PREPARATION

1) Fill a large pot with water and bring to a boil. Lower heat to a simmer and place oranges in the water. Cook for 1 hour
2) Remove stems from cooked oranges, slice in half, and remove any seeds. Place in a food processor and grind until a smooth puree.
3) Preheat oven to 375 degrees
4) Mix chia seeds and water in a large bowl, and let sit until a thick paste is formed.
5) Add remaining ingredients except apples, and mix well.
6) Peel and core apples. Chop to approximate size of ¼ inch cubes. Add to batter and mix well.
7) Spray a 9 inch spring form pan with oil, and pour the batter into the pan. Let sit for 5 minutes.
8) Bake for 55-60 minutes, or until a toothpick inserted comes out clean.
9) Let cake cool, then remove from pan and place onto a serving dish. Chill for several hours.

CAROB CAKE[3]

As always, you have the option of carob or chocolate flavoring; just replace carob powder with cocoa powder for chocolate. Either way, this cake is a sure winner.

INGREDIENTS

4 Tbsp chia seeds
¾ cup very strong coffee
2 cups apple sauce
1 cup sugar
1/3 cup oil
2 tsp apple cider vinegar
¼ cup carob powder
2/3 cup millet flour
2/3 cup brown rice flour
2/3 cup tapioca flour
2 tsp baking soda
½ tsp xanthan gum

Filling
Coconut Whipped Cream recipe (page 71)

Frosting
½ cup coconut butter
2 cups powdered sugar
2 tsp vanilla extract
6 Tbsp carob powder
1/2 cup almond milk

PREPARATION

1) Preheat oven to 375 degrees
2) In a large mixing bowl, combine chia seeds and coffee. Let sit for a few minutes. Stir.
3) Add remaining ingredients and mix well. Stir vigorously for a few seconds.
4) Divide batter between two 9 inch spring form pans which have been sprayed with oil
5) Bake for 25-30 minutes, or until a toothpick comes out clean.
6) Cool layers slightly, remove from pans, and chill.
7) Make coconut whipped cream, spread on bottom cake layer, and place second layer on top.
8) For the frosting, place all ingredients in a saucepan; cook over medium heat while stirring until smooth and syrupy. Remove from heat and allow to cool.
9) Once frosting reaches a good consistency for spreading, frost sides and top of cake. Keep refrigerated.

JELLO POKE CAKE[3]

This is a fun cake, and any flavor of fruit juice can be used for the jello filling. I didn't frost this version, but you can use vanilla buttercream or coconut whipped cream to frost it.

INGREDIENTS

Cake
2 Tbsp ground white chia seeds
½ cup water
¼ cup Earth Balance
½ cup almond milk
¾ cup sugar
2 tsp vanilla extract
1 cup brown rice flour
½ cup arrowroot starch
1 Tbsp baking powder
¼ tsp xanthan gum

Filling
1 cup fruit juice (I used cherry)
2 Tbsp agar agar

PREPARATION

1) Preheat oven to 375 degrees
2) Mix chia seeds and water in a large bowl, and let sit until a thick paste is formed.
3) Add Earth Balance and cream until blended.
4) Add remaining ingredients and mix well. Stir vigorously.
5) Pour batter into an 8 X 8 inch pan which has been sprayed with oil.
6) Bake for 35 minutes, or until a toothpick comes out clean.
7) Let cake cool for about 20 minutes, then make filling.
8) Place fruit juice in a saucepan, and bring to a boil. Lower heat.
9) Whisk in agar agar and continue cooking for 5 minutes, stirring occasionally.
10) Poke holes in cake, evenly spaced, with the handle of a wooden spoon or a large chopstick. Let fruit juice mixture cool for 5 minutes, then pour over the top of the cake.
11) Allow cake to cool, then chill until filling is set.

LAVA CAKE[3]

There are two different methods for making lava cake. One way is to undercook the cake, so the center is still liquid. I chose the second way, where the filling is first frozen, then inserted into the batter before placing the cake in the oven. I chose a vanilla pudding center for contrast.

INGREDIENTS

Cake
2 Tbsp chia seeds
½ cup water
½ cup sugar
¼ cup almond milk
¼ cup oil
2 Tbsp carob powder (or cocoa powder)
1/3 cup buckwheat flour
1/3 cup brown rice flour
1/3 cup tapioca flour
¼ tsp xanthan gum
1 Tbsp baking powder

Filling
1 can coconut milk (chilled overnight)
1 Tbsp kuzu
¼ cup sugar
2 tsp vanilla extract

PREPARATION

1) To make the filling, scoop out thick cream from top of coconut milk, and place in a saucepan.
2) Place kuzu in a small bowl, and add enough of the water from the bottom of the coconut milk can to dissolve the kuzu. Set aside.
3) Add remaining ingredients to the saucepan, and bring to a boil.
4) Lower heat, and add kuzu mixture. Whisk together until smooth – it will begin to thicken. Continue cooking for 5 more minutes, stirring frequently.
5) Cool filling, then pour into an ice cube tray – should make around 9 cubes (you won't need all of them for these cakes). Freeze overnight.
6) Remove frozen filling cubes; they won't come out easily like ice cubes, so you may have to slide a knife around the edges to coax them out. They will be like very hard ice cream. Place them in a plastic bag, and store back in the freezer until ready to use.
7) Preheat oven to 375 degrees
8) In a large mixing bowl, combine chia seeds and water. Let sit for 5 minutes. Stir.
9) Add remaining ingredients and mix well. Stir vigorously to activate xanthan gum.
10) Divide batter between 3 small cake molds which have been sprayed with oil (depending on the size of your molds).
11) Press two filling cubes into the centers of each cake.
12) Bake for 20 minutes, or until a toothpick comes out clean.
13) Allow cakes to cool for 10 to 15 minutes. Invert onto serving dishes, and shake to release them – they should slide right out. Dust with powdered sugar and serve.

MARBLE CAKE[3]

A fun way to combine two different cake flavors. As always, feel free to substitute cocoa for the carob.

INGREDIENTS

6 Tbsp chia seeds
1 ½ cups water
1 cup sugar
2 cups apple sauce
1 Tbsp vanilla extract
2 tsp apple cider vinegar
2 cups white rice flour (+ extra for flouring pan)
1 cup arrowroot starch
2 tsp baking soda
¼ tsp xanthan gum
2 Tbsp unsweetened carob powder
    (or cocoa powder)

PREPARATION

1)   Preheat oven to 375 degrees
2)   In a large mixing bowl, combine chia seeds and water. Let sit for 5 minutes. Stir.
3)   Add remaining ingredients, omitting carob powder. Mix well.
4)   Place 1/3 batter in a separate bowl, and mix with carob powder.
5)   Spoon batter into a tube pan sprayed with oil and floured with rice flour, alternating between the light and the dark batter. With a knife, make swirls through the batter.
6)   Bake for about 1 hour, or until a toothpick comes out clean.
7)   Cool for 10 minutes, and remove cake from pan.

BLUE CAKE[3]

This was laid down as a challenge to me, to mimic a well known bakery cake using only natural ingredients. The signature blue-green frosting doesn't add any special flavor – it's only colored for decoration; so a simple white frosting and filling will taste just as good!

INGREDIENTS

Cake
6 Tbsp chia seeds
1 ½ cups water
1 cup apple sauce
1 cup agave
1/3 cup oil
2 tsp apple cider vinegar
2 cups white rice flour
1 cup tapioca flour
2 tsp baking soda
1 tsp xanthan gum

Filling
Double Coconut Whipped Cream recipe
    (page 71)
Blue coloring (page 69)

Frosting
¼ cup coconut butter
¼ cup coconut oil
3 cups powdered sugar
¼ cup almond milk
Blue coloring (page 69)

PREPARATION

1)   Preheat oven to 375 degrees
2)   In a large mixing bowl, combine chia seeds and water. Let sit for 5 minutes. Stir.
3)   Add remaining ingredients and mix well.
4)   Divide batter between three 9 inch spring form pans which have been sprayed with oil
5)   Bake for 15-20 minutes, or until a toothpick comes out clean.
6)   Cool layers slightly, remove from pans, and chill.
7)   Make coconut whipped cream. Add blue coloring a little at a time until desired color.
8)   Spread half whipped cream on bottom cake layer, and place second layer on top. Spread other half on top, and place last layer on top.
9)   For the frosting, combine all ingredients except almond milk and coloring. Add milk a little at a time until desired consistency. Add coloring a little at a time until desired color.
10) Frost sides and top of cake. Keep refrigerated.

KING CAKE[4]

A must for celebrating Mardi Gras. Though I didn't insert a baby in this one, that can be easily done before baking. These colors are all natural, but standard food coloring can be used to save time.

INGREDIENTS

Dough
¾ cup water
½ cup almond milk
¼ cup sugar
1 packet active dry yeast
2 Tbsp ground chia seeds
1/3 cup Earth Balance
1 tsp apple cider vinegar
1 ½ cups brown rice flour
1 cup millet flour
1 ¾ cups tapioca flour (plus extra for rolling out)
1 tsp xanthan gum

Filling
¼ cup sugar
¼ cup pecans (ground in a food processor)
2 tsp cinnamon
2 Tbsp Earth Balance

Frosting
2 Tbsp Earth Balance
1 ½ cups powdered sugar
3 Tbsp almond milk
1 tsp vanilla extract

Topping
½ cup sugar (divided into thirds)
Purple coloring (page 69)
Pinch of turmeric mixed with a little water
Pinch of spirulina mixed with a little water

PREPARATION

1) Make the colored sugars a few days ahead. Place a little sugar in a plastic bag; add the coloring and shake together until even. Use your fingers to work the coloring into the sugar. The sugar will be damp when you first mix it, so you will need time for it to dry out.
2) For the cake, place ½ cup water, almond milk, and sugar in a medium saucepan. Heat to 105-115 degrees, stirring until sugar is dissolved.
3) Sprinkle yeast on top. Shake pan just until all yeast is covered with liquid. Let sit for 15-20 minutes – contents will more than double in size.
4) Meanwhile, place chia and ¼ cup water in a large bowl. Mix and let sit for 5 minutes or until a thick paste is formed. Cream Earth Balance with the chia mixture and add in vinegar. Mix well.
5) Combine remaining dry ingredients separately, then add to the chia mixture. Mix thoroughly.
6) Form a well in the center, and pour in the yeast mixture. Mix well, then stir vigorously until a soft dough is formed. Add more tapioca flour, a little at a time until you can handle dough without it sticking to your hands.
7) Place dough in a clean bowl, and cover with plastic wrap. Let rise for about one hour – will double in size.
8) Sprinkle tapioca flour generously over a large piece of wax paper placed on a flat surface. Turn the dough onto the paper, and shape into a rectangle. Flour the top with more tapioca flour, place another piece of wax paper on top, and roll out to a 20 X 12 inch rectangle; continually check that you can remove the top paper without it sticking – add more flour if it gets sticky. Keep reshaping edges with your hands to maintain a rectangle shape.
9) Preheat oven to 375 degrees.
10) Make the filling next, by melting the 2 Tbsp Earth Balance; brush the surface of the dough with half the melted butter.
11) Combine sugar, pecans, and cinnamon. Sprinkle evenly on top of the melted butter, leaving ½ inch at the edges.
12) Using the wax paper to guide you, lift up the bottom edge and fold it over onto itself; continue rolling the long edge like a jelly roll. Brush off any excess flour as you go.
13) Cover a cookie sheet with parchment paper, and roll the dough onto the paper seam side down. Bend the ends around to form an oval; pinch the edges of the dough together. Brush the remaining melted butter over the dough.
14) Cover with a large inverted bowl or towel, and let rise for 20-30 minutes.
15) Bake for 15 minutes.
16) Make the frosting by melting Earth Balance in a saucepan over low heat. Add the powdered sugar and almond milk; stir until smooth. Mix in vanilla. Remove from heat.
17) Let frosting cool until it starts to get a little thick. While cake is still warm, pour frosting over the top of the cake, letting it drip down the sides.
18) Sprinkle the colored sugar in stripes around the cake; work quickly because the frosting will harden as it cools.
19) Carefully transfer the cake to a serving dish and serve.

BATTENBERG CAKE[4]

This is a traditional English cake which is as decorative as it is delicious.

INGREDIENTS

Cake
3 Tbsp ground chia
¾ cups water
½ cup apple sauce
½ cup agave
¼ cup oil
1 tsp apple cider vinegar
1 ¼ cups white rice flour
½ cup tapioca flour
1 Tbsp baking powder
1 tsp baking soda
¼ tsp xanthan gum
red food coloring

Apricot Preserves
2 medium apricots
2 Tbsp brown rice syrup
sugar to taste

Frosting
1 Tbsp ground chia
2 Tbsp water
1 cup almond flour
1 ½ cups powdered sugar
2 tsp vanilla extract

PREPARATION

1) Make the apricot preserves first (unless you want to just use canned preserves). Peel and chop the apricots. Place them in a saucepan with brown rice syrup. Cook over medium heat, stirring occasionally, until thick and smooth. Depending on the sweetness of the apricots, you may have to add sugar until the desired sweetness. Allow to cool.
2) Preheat oven to 375 degrees
3) Make the cakes next. To prepare the pan, spray an 8 X 8 inch pan with oil. Create a divider down the middle using aluminum foil folded over several times.
4) In a large bowl, mix the chia and water. Let sit for 5 minutes to thicken.
5) Add remaining ingredients except food coloring, and mix well.
6) Divide batter in half, and add a few drops of red coloring to one half. Pour plain batter on one side of the divider, the pink batter in the other side. Even out batter, and adjust foil if necessary so the center divider is nice and straight. If available, use a cake strip around the pan to prevent excessive doming.
7) Bake for 30-35 minutes, or until a toothpick near the center comes out clean.
8) Let cakes cool. Remove them from the pan, and trim to make them squared off. Slice the tops as well to remove any doming.
9) Slice the cakes in half lengthwise. Assemble pieces into a checkerboard pattern, spread apricot preserves between the pieces.
10) Make the frosting by mixing the chia and water in a bowl; let it sit for a few minutes to thicken.
11) Add flour, sugar, and vanilla, and mix well. Grab the dough with your hands, and knead it together for a couple of minutes until smooth.
12) Flour a piece of wax paper with powdered sugar, and press the marzipan onto the center. Sprinkle more sugar on top, and cover with another piece of wax paper. Roll out in a long rectangle, big enough to cover the sides of the assembled cake (about 7 X 12 inches). Use more sugar if the marzipan gets too sticky.
13) Slice the right edge of the marzipan to be straight. Spread a thin layer of apricot preserves over the top. Place the cake on top of the marzipan, with the seam running down the center of the bottom. Roll the cake and marzipan counter-clockwise, and slice the left edge to the correct length to match up with the first edge. Pinch the seam together, and lay the cake seam side down on a serving dish.
14) Chill for a few hours. Slice the ends off to get a nice, clean edges. Serve.

BANANA BREAD[2]

It's called bread, but this delicious bread makes a great dessert.

INGREDIENTS

2 Tbsp chia seeds

½ cup water

1 can coconut milk (chilled for several days)

3 large bananas (mashed)

½ cup sugar

2 tsp vanilla extract

1/3 cup Earth Balance (melted)

1 cup brown rice flour

½ cup almond flour

½ cup arrowroot starch

1 Tbsp baking powder

½ tsp baking soda

¼ tsp xanthan gum

½ cup walnuts (chopped)

PREPARATION

1) Preheat oven to 375 degrees
2) In a large mixing bowl, combine chia seeds and water. Let sit for a few minutes. Stir.
3) Scoop thick cream from top of coconut milk, and mix with chia.
4) Add remaining ingredients except walnuts, and mix well. Stir vigorously for 30 seconds to activate xanthan gum.
5) Mix in walnuts.
6) Pour batter into a bread pan which has been sprayed with oil.
7) Bake for 50-55 minutes, or until top is browned and firm. Cool and slice.

BANANA PUDDING[3]

This is a southern staple. The vanilla wafers are described in a separate recipe.

INGREDIENTS

2 cans coconut milk
        (left in refrigerator for a few days)

1 Tbsp vanilla extract

½ cup sugar

1/8 tsp turmeric (for color)

¼ cup kuzu

1 cup almond milk

16 Vanilla Wafers (page 117)

2 large bananas (sliced)

Coconut Whipped Cream (page 71)

PREPARATION

1) Open cans of coconut milk and scoop out thick cream from top; place in a large saucepan. Add vanilla, sugar, and turmeric.
2) Place kuzu in a bowl and crush with the back of a fork. Add almond milk and mix until kuzu is fully dissolved.
3) Bring contents of saucepan to a boil, mixing until smooth. Lower heat and whisk in kuzu mixture.
4) Continue cooking for another 5 minutes, stirring frequently. Contents will thicken to a thin pudding.
5) Preheat oven to 350 degrees.
6) Spread vanilla wafers on the bottom of an 8 X 8 inch baking dish.
7) Cover cookies with 1/3 pudding. Spread ½ banana slices on top.
8) Cover banana slices with ½ remaining pudding. Place remaining slices on top, and cover with remaining pudding.
9) Bake for 20 minutes. Cool and chill.
10) Spread coconut whipped cream on top, and pudding is ready to serve.

COCONUT SQUARES[2]

A real treat for coconut lovers. These just use a handful of ingredients.

INGREDIENTS

Crust
5 Medjool Dates (pitted)
2 Tbsp coconut butter
1 ½ cup slivered almonds

Filling
1 cup shredded coconut
2 cans coconut milk (left in fridge for 1-3 days)
1 cup sugar
2 tsp vanilla extract
¼ cup agar agar flakes

PREPARATION

1) Preheat oven to 350 degrees.
2) Place dates and coconut butter in a food processor, and process until a smooth paste is formed. Place the paste in a bowl.
3) Pulse the almonds in a food processor until ground. Add to the date paste and mix well.
4) Press the almond mixture onto the bottom of an 8 X 8 inch square baking dish which has been sprayed with oil. Even it out and press it down firmly with your hands.
5) Bake for 15 minutes.
6) To make the filling, toast the coconut by spreading evenly over a cookie sheet covered with parchment paper. Bake for 3 minutes, mix shreds, then bake for another 2 minutes.
7) Open the coconut milk cans and scoop out the thick cream from the top; place in a saucepan.
8) Add ¾ cup of the coconut shreds, sugar, and vanilla. Stir and bring to a boil.
9) Lower heat and whisk in agar agar flakes. Continue cooking for 5 minutes, stirring occasionally.
10) Let cool slightly, then pour over the baked crust. Sprinkle remaining coconut shreds on top and let cool.
11) Chill until set, then cut into squares. Makes 36 squares.

COCONUT FLAN[3]

Yes, you truly CAN have a vegan flan. The coconut cream gives a really rich flavor and creamy consistency. Adjust the quantity of agar agar if you like – less for a softer flan, or more for a firmer one.

INGREDIENTS

1 ¼ cups raw sugar (preferably dark)
¼ cup water
2 cans coconut milk
    (left in refrigerator for a few days)
1 cup almond milk
1 tsp vanilla extract
¼ cup agar agar flakes

PREPARATION

1) Preheat oven to 350 degrees.
2) Dissolve ¾ cup sugar in the water over medium heat. Continue cooking until liquid turns dark and begins to thicken. Be sure not to cook too fast or the sugar will burn.
3) Pour the liquid into six ¾ cup ramekins, quickly swirling to cover bottom and sides.
4) Scoop out the hard coconut cream from the top of the coconut milk cans and place into a saucepan. Add almond milk, vanilla, and remaining sugar. Bring to a boil, stirring occasionally.
5) Lower heat and whisk in the agar agar. Continue cooking for 5 minutes, stirring occasionally.
6) Place ramekins in a large baking dish, and divide the liquid from the saucepan amongst them. Pour water into the baking dish until it is half way up the sides of the ramekins. Bake for 20 minutes.
7) Cool ramekins and chill for at least an hour or until set.
8) To serve, loosen the edges of the flan with a knife, and invert onto a plate. Holding the ramekin firmly on the plate, shake hard until you hear the flan slide out of the ramekin. Remove the ramekin and serve.

STRAWBERRY SHORTCAKE[3]

In my first book I had a recipe for a single large cake, but this is the more traditional southern style with a biscuit. And, of course, it's also vegan.

INGREDIENTS

Biscuits

1 Tbsp ground chia
¼ cup water
¼ cup + 1 tsp Earth Balance
2 Tbsp sugar
1/3 cup brown rice flour
2/3 cups tapioca flour (plus extra for rolling out)
2 tsp baking powder
¼ tsp xanthan gum

Topping

1 cup chopped strawberries
1 Tbsp sugar
Coconut Whipped Cream (page 71)

PREPARATION

1) For the biscuits, mix chia and water; let sit for a few minutes until thick.
2) Cream in ¼ cup Earth Balance and sugar. Mix well.
3) Add remaining dry ingredients, and mix well. Stir vigorously to form a soft dough. Knead the dough for a few minutes; add more tapioca flour if too sticky. Chill for 30 minutes
4) Preheat oven to 425 degrees.
5) Lightly flour a piece of wax paper with tapioca flour. Press dough onto paper, and form into a 5 X 5 inch square.
6) With a sharp knife, cut the dough into 4 2 ½ inch squares.
7) Cover a cookie sheet with parchment paper, and transfer the dough squares onto the sheet. Indent the tops with a finger.
8) Melt remaining Earth Balance, and brush the tops of the biscuits with the melted butter.
9) Bake for 5 minutes; turn over and bake for another 3 minutes or until the bottoms are golden.
10) Cool biscuits, then slice in half horizontally.
11) Mix the strawberries with the sugar, and let sit for 10-15 minutes.
12) To assemble the shortcakes, spoon strawberries onto the biscuit bottom; cover with whipped cream, followed by the top of the biscuit. Spoon more whipped cream on top, then spoon more strawberries on top. Makes 4 shortcakes.

PEANUT BUTTER HALVAH[3]

I grew up eating traditional sesame halvah. This is a great twist for peanut butter lovers.

INGREDIENTS

1 cup peanut butter
1 cup sugar
¼ cup water

PREPARATION

1) Place peanut butter in a mixing bowl. Have a mixer ready to go with a paddle attachment, and a piece of wax paper.
2) Place sugar and water in a saucepan. Heat over medium heat to dissolve sugar. Continue cooking until dark and syrupy (temperature should reach 248 degrees).
3) Slowly pour the melted sugar over the peanut butter, mixing at low speed. Mix just enough for everything to be evenly blended.
4) Pour contents onto wax paper and spread to form a 6 X 6 inch square. Fold edges of paper up and over the top to form a neat, firm package. Flip over so open edges are on the bottom. Let cool slightly, then chill to harden.
5) If desired, cut into small squares.

FIG NEWTONS[4]

Fresh figs make these cookies absolutely delicious. There are a large number of different figs to choose from – each with a unique flavor. These use black figs, but any type will do.

INGREDIENTS

Dough
1 Tbsp ground white chia seeds
¼ cup water
½ cup Earth Balance
¼ cup dark sugar
¼ cup brown rice syrup
¾ cup brown rice flour
¾ cup millet flour
¾ cup tapioca flour (plus extra for rolling out)
½ tsp xanthan gum
1 tsp orange peel

Filling
1 lb black figs
½ cup sugar
¼ tsp cinnamon

PREPARATION

1) Make the filling first. Remove fig stems, and place figs in a saucepan with 2-3 cups water. Heat covered over low heat for 45 minutes.
2) Drain figs and place in a food processor with sugar and cinnamon. Grind until smooth.
3) Return puree to saucepan, and cook over low heat for 30 minutes (or until thick), stirring frequently.
4) To make the dough, combine the chia and water in a bowl and let sit for 5 minutes or until thick. Cream Earth Balance and sugar with the chia mixture. Add brown rice syrup and mix well.
5) Combine dry ingredients separately, and add to the wet ingredients. Mix well and stir vigorously until a sticky dough is formed. Work in extra tapioca flour until the dough doesn't stick to your hands. Break into 4 balls and chill for 30 minutes.
6) Preheat oven to 375 degrees.
7) You will need two small widths of wax paper (about 6 inches). Cover a cookie sheet with parchment paper, and set aside. On a flat surface, flour about a 3 ½ inch width of each piece of wax paper.
8) Take one of the dough balls, and work it with your hands into a long sausage shape (12 inches long). Press into the center of the wax paper and flatten it with your hands. Place the other piece on top, floured side down, and roll the dough to about 3 ½ inches in width. Remove the paper, and square everything off with your hands; you want to end up with a nice even 3 ½ X 12 inch rectangle.
9) Using a knife, spread the fig filling along the center of the rectangle about 1 inch wide and ¼ inch high. Even it out over the length of the dough.
10) Using the paper as a guide, fold the right side of the dough up and over the filling; continue rolling the dough over so the seam is on the bottom;
11) Carefully lift the roll with the paper, and place it on top of the parchment paper on the cookie sheet; Slide the roll off of the wax paper and onto the parchment paper. Even out the shape with your hands, and flatten it a bit.
12) Continue process for 3 remaining balls of dough. Use a pastry brush to brush any excess flour from the rolls.
13) Bake for 15 minutes. Slice the ends off the rolls, then slice into 1 ½ inch lengths. Makes 32 cookies.

RUGELACH[5]

These decorative cookies take a little practice to master; the results are not only visually impressive, but delicious as well.

INGREDIENTS

Dough

2 Tbsp ground chia seeds
¼ cup water
½ cup Earth Balance
4 oz Daiya plain cream cheese
¼ cup sugar
¾ cup brown rice flour
¾ cup millet flour
½ tsp xanthan gum
¾ cup tapioca flour (plus extra for rolling out)

Filling

¾ cup medjool dates (around 9 – pitted)
¾ cup sugar
1/3 cup water
¼ cup carob powder
      (can use cocoa powder if preferred)

PREPARATION

1) Place the ground chia seeds and water in a bowl and stir. Let sit for a few minutes until thick.
2) Cream in Earth Balance, cream cheese, and sugar.
3) Add rice flour, millet flour, and xanthan gum. Mix together, and stir vigorously to activate xanthan gum.
4) Mix in tapioca flour to form a soft dough.
5) Divide into quarters, wrap each piece in plastic wrap, and chill for 30 minutes.
6) Make filling by placing all ingredients in a food processor; process until a smooth paste is formed.
7) Preheat oven to 350 degrees.
8) Remove a section of dough from the refrigerator; warm slightly and flatten in your hands. Dip into tapioca flour to cover the bottom.
9) Press onto a piece of wax paper, and flatten to a 6 inch circle with your hands; work the edges with your fingers to keep it as round as possible.
10) Generously flour the top of the dough with tapioca flour; place another piece of wax paper on top, slide your hand underneath the bottom paper, and flip the dough over sandwiched between the two sheets of paper.
11) Peel off the top paper, flour the top of the dough, and return the paper on top. Carefully roll out the dough to a 9 inch circle. Remove the top paper, and use your hands to shape the dough so the circle is even and round.
12) Spread a thin layer of the filling over the dough, almost to the edges.
13) Using a sharp knife, slice the dough like a pie into 16 narrow triangles. When cutting the dough, do not slide the knife vertically through the dough; rather, push the knife down to cut the dough, then roll it back up to remove it. The dough will have a tendency to stick to the knife, so cut it very carefully to keep the shape intact.
14) To form each cookie, take a dinner knife, flour it with some tapioca flour, and slide it all the way underneath a triangle of dough. Gently life and slide it out to move the triangle to an open section of the paper. Now you will be able to roll it, beginning with the wide edge; keep the roll as tight as possible, and roll toward the tip of the triangle. Place the finished roll, point side down, onto a cookie sheet lined with parchment paper.
15) Continue rolling out dough, spreading filling, cutting, and rolling up, until all sections have been used.
16) Bake for 15 minutes – bottoms should be just browned. Makes 64 cookies.

CAROB CHIPS[2]

I looked for vegan/gluten-free carob chips in the store, but they were impossible to find – so I decided to make them myself. Chocolate might be easier, but still difficult to find.

INGREDIENTS

½ cup sugar
½ cup carob powder (or cocoa powder)
2 tsp vanilla extract
½ cup water
1 cup coconut butter

PREPARATION

1) Place all ingredients except coconut butter in a saucepan. Heat over low heat and stir until the sugar melts and consistency is smooth. Remove from heat.
2) In another saucepan, heat coconut butter over low heat until completely melted and smooth.
3) Add coconut butter to carob mixture, and mix well. Turn onto a sheet of parchment paper, and spread to a rectangle about ¼ inch thick. Allow to cool.
4) Chill until solid but not too hard. Slice with a sharp knife into ¼ inch squares.
5) Continue to chill until fully hardened. Break apart. Makes about 2 cups.

CAROB CHIP COOKIES[2]

Once you make the carob chips in the recipe above, it's pretty easy to make these classic cookies.

INGREDIENTS

1 Tbsp ground chia seeds
¼ cup water
1 tsp vanilla extract
½ cup Earth Balance
¾ cup sugar
2/3 cup almond flour
2/3 cup brown rice flour
1/3 cup millet flour
1/3 cup tapioca flour
½ tsp baking powder
1 cup carob chips (frozen)

PREPARATION

1) Preheat oven to 350 degrees.
2) Place the ground chia seeds and water in a bowl and stir. Let sit for a few minutes until thick.
3) Mix in vanilla extract. Cream in Earth Balance and sugar until well mixed.
4) Add remaining ingredients except for carob chips. Mix well.
5) Mix in carob chips and chill for 30 minutes.
6) Drop by spoonfuls onto a cookie sheet covered with parchment paper, leaving plenty of room for spreading. Flatten cookies.
7) Bake for around 17-18 minutes, until edges are brown. Makes 3-4 dozen.

ECLAIRS[4]

There are lots of possibilities for filling and frosting flavors – these have a vanilla cream filling and carob frosting.

INGREDIENTS

Puff Paste
Liquid from 1 15 oz can garbanzo beans
         (aquafaba)
¼ tsp cream of tartar
1/3 cup brown rice flour
1/3 cup millet flour
1/3 cup arrowroot starch
¼ cup sugar
1 Tbsp baking powder
¼ tsp xanthan gum
1 cup almond milk
¼ cup Earth Balance

Filling
1 can coconut milk (chilled overnight)
¼ cup sugar
2 tsp vanilla extract
Pinch turmeric (for color)
3 Tsp kuzu

Frosting
2 Tbsp coconut butter
¾ cup powdered sugar
2 Tbsp carob powder (can use cocoa powder)
1 tsp vanilla extract
1 ½ Tbsp almond milk

PREPARATION

1) Make the filling first. Scoop the thick cream from the top of the can of coconut milk. Place in a saucepan with the sugar, vanilla extract, and turmeric. Do not discard water from can.
2) In a small bowl, crush the kuzu and mix with a little of the water from the coconut milk can to form a paste.
3) Bring the contents of the saucepan to a boil. Lower heat and mix in the kuzu paste. Cook for 5 minutes, stirring frequently. Let cool, then chill, stirring occasionally during the process.
4) To make the puff paste, place the liquid from the garbanzo beans in a small saucepan. Cook over medium heat until cooked down to approximately 1/3 cup.
5) Preheat oven to 400 degrees.
6) Let the liquid cool for a few minutes; add the cream of tartar and beat at high speed until stiff (about 5 minutes). It will look like stiff beaten egg whites.
7) Combine the remaining dry ingredients in a bowl.
8) In a medium saucepan, combine the almond milk and Earth Balance and bring to a boil.
9) Lower the heat to a simmer and add the dry ingredients all at once. Whisk together until a dough is formed which starts to pull away from the sides.
10) Remove from heat and allow to cool slightly. Mix in the beaten aquafaba a little at a time. Stir vigorously to activate xanthan gum.
11) Cover a cookie sheet with parchment paper (or, better yet, a silicone baking sheet), and pipe with a ½ - ¾ inch tip to form éclair shapes 5 inches long.
12) Bake on top rack for 20 minutes (best to leave an empty cookie sheet on a lower rack to keep bottoms from burning). Lower temperature to 350 and bake for another 15 minutes. Shells should be golden in color.
13) Let shells cool, then slice in half horizontally with a sharp knife, and flip the top halves over. Scoop out dough from both halves with a small spoon and discard.
14) Pipe the filling into the top half, then flip the bottom over and place on top. Turn éclair over so the flat side is on the bottom.
15) For the frosting, place all ingredients in a saucepan and heat over low heat; stir constantly until a good consistency. Spread warm frosting on top of each éclair, and allow to cool completely. Makes one dozen.

MACARONS[5]

This is known as one of the most difficult pastries to make in traditional baking. I've worked hard to perfect this recipe, and if you follow it precisely you will have delicious, perfect cookies every time. This recipe is for raspberry, but I also have a simple modification for carob (or chocolate).

INGREDIENTS

Shells

1 15 oz can garbanzo beans
¼ tsp cream of tartar
Few drops of red food coloring (optional)
1 ½ cups powdered sugar
1 cup almond flour
(for carob/chocolate, replace food coloring with
    2 Tbsp carob/cocoa powder)

Filling

½ cup raspberries
¼ cup water
¼ cup Earth Balance
1 cup powdered sugar
(for carob/chocolate, replace raspberry syrup
    with 2 Tbsp carob/cocoa powder and
    2 Tbsp almond milk)

PREPARATION

1) Drain liquid (aquafaba) from garbanzo beans. Place 1/3 cup in a bowl (save remaining liquid for other recipes).
2) Add cream of tartar to liquid in bowl. Beat at high speed until soft peaks form.
3) If desired, add a few drops of red food coloring, and beat until smooth.
4) Add 1 cup sugar a little at a time while continuing to beat mixture. Continue beating until very stiff.
5) Sift together remaining sugar and almond flour. Fold into aquafaba mixture until fully incorporated and consistency is smooth (roughly 60 turns). Consistency should be like flowing lava.
6) Cover 2 cookies sheets with parchment paper. Place batter into a pastry bag, and pipe onto the paper to form 1 ½ inch circles spaced well apart. Use a plain tip which is not too big – ¼ inch works well (if the tip is too big it becomes difficult to control). Bang cookie sheets onto flat surface several times to release any air bubbles.
7) Preheat oven to 275 degrees.
8) Let shells sit for 20 minutes. Surface should look dry and dull. Bake one sheet at a time for 20 minutes. Cool.
9) To make the filling, puree the raspberries and water in a food processor. Run through a strainer to remove the seeds, and place the seedless puree into a small saucepan. Cook until a thick syrup is formed. Allow to fully cool.
10) Cream the Earth Balance and raspberry syrup together. Add sugar and mix until smooth.
11) Chill filling until the consistency of frosting. For half of the shells, spread the filling on the flat side, sandwiching another shell on top; Press the shells together and twist until filling spreads to the edges.
12) Chill the cookies for a couple of hours to allow the filling to harden. Makes about 2 dozen sandwiches.

BANANA NUT COOKIES[2]

Just like having banana bread but in a cookie. Once you start eating these, it's hard to stop.

INGREDIENTS

1 Tbsp ground chia seeds
¼ cup water
½ cup Earth Balance
½ cup sugar
1 cup mashed bananas (2-3 bananas)
1 cup brown rice flour
1 cup almond flour
½ cup tapioca flour
½ tsp baking soda
1 cup walnuts(chopped)

PREPARATION

1) Preheat oven to 375 degrees.
2) Place the ground chia seeds and water in a bowl and stir. Let sit for a few minutes until thick.
3) Cream in Earth Balance and sugar until well mixed.
4) Add remaining ingredients except for walnuts. Mix well.
5) Mix in walnuts.
6) Drop by spoonfuls onto a cookie sheet covered with parchment paper, leaving room for spreading. Flatten cookies.
7) Bake for around 15 minutes, until edges are brown. Makes 3 ½ - 4 dozen.

DATE WALNUT COOKIES[2]

Dates and walnuts go together so perfectly, but pecans can be used as well.

INGREDIENTS

2 cups medjool dates (pitted)
1 Tbsp ground chia
¼ cup water
½ cup Earth Balance
2 tsp vanilla extract
½ cup quinoa flour
½ cup brown rice flour
½ cup arrowroot starch
1 tsp baking powder
1 cup walnuts

PREPARATION

1) Preheat oven to 350 degrees.
2) Place dates in a food processor, and grind until a smooth paste is formed. Set aside.
3) In a bowl, combine chia and water. Let sit for a few minutes until thick.
4) Cream Earth Balance into the chia mixture.
5) Add date paste and remaining ingredients except walnuts, and mix well.
6) Chop walnuts and add to the batter. Mix well.
7) Cover a cookie sheet with parchment paper. With your hands, roll batter into 1 inch balls and place on the paper. Flatten to 2 inch discs.
8) Bake for 12-14 minutes or until the edges begin to brown. Makes about 4 dozen.

LEMON SANDWICH COOKIES[3]

The combination of lemon and coconut makes these stand out from other lemon cookies.

INGREDIENTS

1 Tbsp ground chia seeds

¼ cup water

2 tsp vanilla extract

½ cup Earth Balance

1 cup sugar

1 cup brown rice flour

¾ cup millet flour

¾ cup tapioca flour (plus extra for rolling out)

¼ tsp xanthan gum

Filling

½ cup coconut butter

3 Tbsp lemon juice

3 Tbsp almond milk

2 cups powdered sugar

PREPARATION

1) Place the ground chia seeds and water in a bowl and stir. Let sit for a few minutes until thick.
2) Mix in vanilla extract. Cream in Earth Balance until well mixed.
3) Add remaining ingredients and mix until a dough is formed. Work dough with your hands until smooth. Chill for 30 minutes.
4) Preheat oven to 375 degrees.
5) Take half the dough, cover it with tapioca flour, and press it onto the paper. Flatten it with your hands to form a rectangle. Sprinkle more flour on the top and on the paper, place another piece of wax paper on top, and roll out to about 1/16 inch thickness. Remove the top paper.
6) Using a small glass (about 2-2.5 inch diameter) or cookie cutter, cut dough into circles. Remove excess dough and place back into refrigerator. Using a small spatula, place dough circles onto a cookie sheet covered with parchment paper. Cut each circle in half with a sharp knife, and move the halves away from each other to allow room for spreading.
7) Bake for around 10 minutes, until edges are golden.
8) Repeat with remaining half of dough, and continue rolling out discarded dough until all dough has been used.
9) Once cookies have cooled completely, make filling by placing the coconut butter in a saucepan. Heat over low heat until melted, then add remaining ingredients; stir until a smooth consistency.
10) Spread filling on the bottom of one half-circle, and place the other half-circle on top, bottom side down. Press together slightly, and wipe off excess filling with your finger. Allow filling to harden before serving. Makes around 4 dozen.

PEANUT BUTTER SANDWICH COOKIES[3]

A peanut butter lover's dream. Always use freshly ground peanut butter for the best flavor. Almond butter can be substituted if you're not a peanut butter fan, but I've found almond butter needs a little less sugar.

INGREDIENTS

1 Tbsp ground chia

¼ cup water

½ cup Earth Balance

1 cup sugar

1 tsp vanilla extract

2/3 cup millet flour

2/3 cup brown rice flour

1/3 cup tapioca flour

½ tsp baking powder

1 cup peanut butter

Filling

½ cup peanut butter

1 cup powdered sugar

2-4 Tbsp almond milk

PREPARATION

1) In a bowl, combine chia and water. Let sit for a few minutes until thick.
2) Cream Earth Balance into the chia mixture.
3) Add remaining ingredients except peanut butter, and mix well.
4) Stir in the peanut butter until combined. Chill for 30 minutes
5) Preheat oven to 375 degrees.
6) Roll batter into ¾ inch balls and place on a cookie sheet covered with parchment paper, leaving space between the balls.
7) Flatten balls with your fingers to 2 inch discs. Stamp with a potato masher (if available), or make a criss cross pattern with a fork.
8) Bake for 9-10 minutes or until the edges turn golden.
9) To make the filling, combine the peanut butter and sugar. Add almond milk a little at a time until a good consistency for spreading.
10) Spread filling roughly on the bottom of a cookie. Place another cookie on top, bottom side down; press and turn the top cookie until the filling seeps out at the edges. Wipe off excess filling with your finger. Continue with remaining pairs of cookies. Makes about 3 dozen.

MANDARIN ORANGE COOKIES[2]

The tart flavor of mandarin oranges makes these cookies unique. Regular oranges could be used as well, but they won't be quite as special.

INGREDIENTS

3 small mandarin oranges (about 1/3 lb)
1 Tbsp ground chia seeds
¼ cup water
1/3 cup oil
½ cup sugar
1 cup almond flour
½ cup arrowroot starch

Frosting
1 cup powdered sugar
Juice from 2 small mandarin oranges

PREPARATION

1) Fill a pot with water and bring to a boil. Drop 3 oranges in the water and cook over low heat for 1 hour.
2) Allow oranges to cool, then remove any remaining piece of stems, slice in half, and remove any seeds. Place in a food processor and grind until smooth.
3) Preheat oven to 350 degrees.
4) Place the ground chia seeds and water in a bowl and stir. Let sit for a few minutes until thick.
5) Add orange puree and remaining ingredients, and stir well.
6) Cover a baking sheet with parchment paper, and drop batter by teaspoonfuls onto paper (leave space for spreading). Flatten cookies.
7) Bake for 15-17 minutes, until the edges start to brown.
8) Once cookies are completely cooled, make the frosting by stirring the juice into the sugar a little at a time; add juice until the frosting is a good consistency for frosting.
9) Frost the tops of the cookies, and allow the frosting to harden. Makes 3-4 dozen.

RASPBERRY THUMBPRINT COOKIES[3]

Any fruit can be used for the filling – you can even use store bought jam if you want to save the work of making it yourself.

INGREDIENTS

1 Tbsp ground chia seeds
¼ cup water
2 tsps vanilla extract
½ cup Earth Balance
¾ cup sugar
1 cup brown rice flour
¾ cup millet flour
¾ cup tapioca flour
¼ tsp baking powder

Jam
1 ½ cups raspberries
3 Tbsp brown rice syrup

PREPARATION

1) Make the jam first. Place raspberries in a food processor and grind until smooth.
2) Run raspberry puree through a strainer to remove the seeds. Place in a saucepan with brown rice syrup and cook over medium heat until thick – about 30 minutes. Be sure to stir frequently as you get toward the end, or it will burn.
3) Cool jam and chill.
4) Preheat oven to 375 degrees.
5) Place the ground chia seeds and water in a bowl and stir. Let sit for a few minutes until thick.
6) Mix in vanilla extract. Cream in Earth Balance and sugar until well mixed.
7) Add remaining ingredients. Mix well.
8) Cover a baking sheet with parchment paper. Roll 1 inch balls of dough with your hands and place on the baking sheet with plenty of room for spreading.
9) Flatten balls slightly. Depress the centers with your thumb.
10) Spoon jam on centers of cookies. Bake for 13-15 minutes, or until bottoms turn golden. Makes about 3 dozen.

MAPLE PECAN COOKIES[2]

These cookies combine the flavors of maple syrup and pecans; they're almost like eating pancakes in a cookie form.

INGREDIENTS

1 Tbsp ground chia seeds
¼ cup water
1 tsp vanilla extract
½ cup Earth Balance
¾ cup maple syrup
1 cup brown rice flour
2/3 cup almond flour
1/3 cup arrowroot starch
½ tsp baking powder
1 cup pecans (chopped)

PREPARATION

1) Preheat oven to 375 degrees.
2) Place the ground chia seeds and water in a bowl and stir. Let sit for a few minutes until thick.
3) Mix in vanilla extract. Cream in Earth Balance until well mixed.
4) Add remaining ingredients except for pecans. Mix well.
5) Mix in pecans, and chill for 30 minutes.
6) Drop by spoonfuls onto a cookie sheet covered with parchment paper, leaving plenty of room for spreading. Flatten cookies.
7) Bake for around 12-14 minutes, until edges are brown. Makes 3-4 dozen.

SESAME SEED COOKIES[3]

These cookies were inspired by Chinese sesame balls

INGREDIENTS

1 Tbsp ground chia seeds
¼ cup water
1/3 cup oil
¼ cup almond milk
1 cup sugar
1 cup almond flour
½ cup arrowroot starch
¼ cup coconut flour
1 tsp baking powder
½ cup sesame seeds

PREPARATION

1) Preheat oven to 375 degrees.
2) Place the ground chia seeds and water in a bowl and stir. Let sit for a few minutes until thick.
3) Add remaining ingredients except for the sesame seeds, and mix well.
4) Cover a cookie sheet with parchment paper, and roll the dough into one inch balls. Place the balls on the cookie sheet with plenty of space in between them.
5) Place the sesame seeds in a bowl; one by one, take each ball and roll it in the sesame seeds until completely covered; then place the ball back onto the cookie sheet.
6) Flatten each ball with your fingers to form a round cookie shape about 1/8 inch thick.
7) Bake for 7-8 minutes, until the bottoms are golden brown.
8) Turn each cookie over, and continue baking for another 2-3 minutes to brown the other sides. Makes about 3 dozen.

MILANO COOKIES[3]

These can be particularly addictive, and well worth the amount of work to make them.

INGREDIENTS

½ cup Earth Balance
1 ½ cups powdered sugar
2/3 cup aquafaba (liquid from can of chickpeas)
2 tsp vanilla extract
1 cup brown rice flour
1 cup millet flour
2/3 cup tapioca flour

Filling
¼ cup Earth Balance
3 Tbsp carob powder (or cocoa powder)
2 Tbsp almond milk
1 cup powdered sugar

PREPARATION

1) Preheat oven to 350 degrees.
2) Cream the Earth Balance, then add remaining ingredients. Mix until smooth.
3) Cover a cookie sheet with parchment paper. Pour the batter into a pastry bag with a ¼ inch tip. Pipe batter onto paper in 3 inch strips, leaving plenty of room for spreading.
4) Bake for around 14 minutes, or until edges just start to turn golden.
5) Continue piping and baking for remainder of the batter. Allow cookies to completely cool.
6) For the filling, cream the Earth Balance, then add remaining ingredients. Mix until smooth.
7) Spread filling onto flat side of cookie; place another cookie on top of the filling, flat side down. Press the cookies together until the filling begins to ooze out the edges.
8) Chill cookies until filling hardens. Makes about 4 dozen sandwiches.

SHORTBREAD COOKIES[2]

You can make these unfrosted, but half dipped they not only look better, but taste better too.

INGREDIENTS

1 cup Earth Balance
½ cup sugar
1 Tbsp vanilla extract
1 1/3 cup brown rice flour
1 ¼ cup tapioca flour (plus extra for rolling out)
½ tsp xanthan gum

Frosting
1 cup powdered sugar
2 Tbsp unsweetened carob powder
      (or cocoa powder)
3-4 Tbsp almond milk

PREPARATION

1) Preheat oven to 350 degrees.
2) Cream Earth Balance and sugar until smooth
3) Mix in vanilla extract
4) Separately combine remaining dry ingredients, and add to Earth Balance mixture. Stir until a soft dough is formed. If dough is sticky, work in more tapioca flour until dough stops sticking.
5) Chill dough for 30 minutes
6) Flour a piece of wax paper with tapioca flour. Roll dough in flour, and press onto center of paper. Shape into a rectangle with your hands, and flour the top.
7) Place another piece of wax paper on top, and roll to a ½ inch thick rectangle.
8) Using a pastry cutter and a straight edge (or a cookie cutter if you have one), cut into 1 ½ inch squares. Place squares onto a cookie sheet covered with parchment paper. Gather up leftover dough, and continue rolling out and cutting until all dough is used up.
9) Chill cookie sheet for 30 minutes.
10) Bake for 15 minutes, or until bottoms are browned.
11) Make frosting by combining dry ingredients. Add almond milk a little at a time, until a good consistency for dipping. Dip cooled cookies into frosting, and place back onto parchment paper to dry. Makes 4-5 dozen.

CARROT COOKIES[2]

Carrots don't have to only be for cake – they are great in cookies as well.

INGREDIENTS

1 Tbsp ground chia seeds
¼ cup water
2 large carrots
1 tsp vanilla
½ cup Earth Balance
½ cup sugar
¾ cup brown rice flour
¾ cup millet flour
½ cup arrowroot starch
1 tsp baking powder

Frosting
1 cup powdered sugar
2-3 Tbsp orange juice

PREPARATION

1) Preheat oven to 375 degrees.
2) Place the ground chia seeds and water in a bowl and stir. Let sit for a few minutes until thick.
3) Peel and coarsely chop carrots. Place in a food processor and pulse until finely chopped (about 1 cup). Add to chia mixture and stir.
4) Mix in vanilla extract. Cream Earth Balance and mix in. Add remaining ingredients and mix until even. Chill for 30 minutes.
5) Cover a cookie sheet with parchment paper, and drop batter by tablespoonfuls spaced well apart. Flatten to 2 ½ inch discs.
6) Bake for 16-18 minutes, until the bottoms are golden brown.
7) When cookies have cooled, make frosting by adding orange juice to sugar a little at a time until a thick glaze is formed. Drizzle over cookies (use a squeeze bottle for a fancier appearance). Allow frosting to harden. Makes 4 dozen.

VANILLA WAFERS[2]

I developed these specifically to be used in banana pudding, but they are great on their own as well.

INGREDIENTS

1 Tbsp ground chia seeds
¼ cup water
4 tsps vanilla extract
½ cup Earth Balance
½ cup sugar
2/3 cup brown rice flour
2/3 cup millet flour
2/3 cup tapioca flour
½ tsp baking powder

PREPARATION

1) Preheat oven to 375 degrees.
2) Place the ground chia seeds and water in a bowl and stir. Let sit for a few minutes until thick.
3) Mix in vanilla extract. Cream in Earth Balance and sugar until well mixed.
4) Add remaining ingredients. Mix well.
5) Chill for 30 minutes.
6) Cover a baking sheet with parchment paper. Grab teasponfuls of batter with your fingers, and press onto the paper into slightly flattened, 1 inch diameter disks. Leave room for spreading.
7) Bake for around 13-15 minutes, until edges are brown. Makes about 5 dozen.

FORTUNE COOKIES[5]

You can have a lot of fun making up your own fortunes. Print out your own slips of paper and insert them into these delicious cookies. You can also leave out the fortunes and just enjoy the cookies.

INGREDIENTS

½ cup + 2 Tbsp white rice flour
2 Tbsp tapioca flour
1/3 cup sugar
6 Tbsp aquafaba (liquid from a can of chickpeas)
2 Tbsp oil
1 Tbsp water
1 tsp vanilla extract

PREPARATION

1) Preheat oven to 375 degrees. Have preprinted fortunes ready.
2) In a mixing bowl, combine all ingredients. Beat at high speed for 2 minutes.
3) Cover a cookie sheet with a silicone mat. Drop batter onto mat by Tbsp-fuls, only making 4 at one time. Spread each cookie with a knife to a 3 – 3 ½ inch circle.
4) Bake for 8 minutes, or until edges start to turn golden.
5) This part needs to be done quickly, before the cookies cool. First, loosen each cookie with a spatula.
6) For each cookie, lay a fortune across the center, and fold the cookie in half so that the edges meet. While still holding the edges together, round edges pointing upward, press the folded edge down against a cup rim or the edge of the cookie sheet to bend the corners toward each other. Place the cookie in a muffin pan to maintain the shape.
7) Once all 4 cookies have been shaped, go back and press the edges together if they have separated. Until the cookies cool, they will remain pliable. Once they have cooled enough to maintain their shape, move on to the next batch of 4. Makes around 20 cookies.

SNICKERDOODLES[2]

A treat for cinnamon lovers. These light cookies rolled in sugar and cinnamon will literally melt in your mouth.

INGREDIENTS

1 Tbsp ground chia seeds
¼ cup water
½ cup Earth Balance
½ cup + 3 Tbsp sugar
½ cup almond flour
½ cup brown rice flour
½ cup millet flour
½ cup tapioca flour
1 tsp baking powder
1 ½ tsp cinnamon

PREPARATION

1) Place the ground chia seeds and water in a bowl and stir. Let sit for a few minutes until thick.
2) Cream in Earth Balance and ½ cup sugar until well mixed.
3) Add remaining ingredients except for 3 Tbsp sugar and cinnamon; mix well. Chill for 30 minutes.
4) Preheat oven to 375 degrees.
5) In a small bowl, combine 3 Tbsp sugar and cinnamon.
6) Cover a cookie sheet with parchment paper. Roll cookie dough into 1 inch balls, then roll in the sugar/cinnamon mixture to coat. Place on cookie sheet leaving plenty of room for spreading, and flatten slightly.
7) Bake for 9-11 minutes, or until bottoms are browned. Makes 3 dozen.

CHECKERBOARD COOKIES[5]

These are a variation of shortbread cookies. They are fun to make, but take some practice to handle the delicate dough. Even if the dough breaks, however, it will all just melt together when it bakes.

INGREDIENTS

1 cup Earth Balance
½ cup sugar
1 Tbsp vanilla extract
1 1/3 cup brown rice flour
½ tsp xanthan gum
3 Tbsp carob powder (or cocoa powder)
1 cup tapioca flour (plus extra for finishing)

PREPARATION

1) Cream Earth Balance and sugar in a bowl until smooth
2) Mix in vanilla extract
3) Mix in brown rice flour and xanthan gum. Stir vigorously for a minute.
4) Take a little less than half the dough (4/9) and place in a separate bowl.
5) Add carob powder to first bowl, and mix well.
6) To each bowl, work in ½ cup tapioca flour. Add extra flour a little at a time until dough gets a little dry and crackly. The carob bowl will need a little less, since the carob powder dries it out a little.
7) Divide each type of dough into two halves, and chill for 10-15 minutes.
8) Cover two cookie sheets in parchment paper, and preheat oven to 350 degrees.
9) Flour a piece of wax paper lightly with tapioca flour. Take half of the white dough, and use your hands to shape it into a rectangle which is 7 ½ inches long by 2 inches wide (will be about ½ inch high). Using a sharp knife, slice the dough horizontally into four ½ inch wide strips.
10) On a separate section of the paper, shape half of the brown dough into a 7 ½ X 2 ½ inch rectangle. Slice it horizontally into five ½ inch wide strips.
11) Using a thin spatula to help you, arrange the strips as follows: on the bottom layer, alternating with 1 brown, 1 white, and 1 brown strip. Above that, 1 white, 1 brown, and 1 white strip. On the top, 1 brown, 1 white, and 1 brown strip. Press the block together with your hands, and use the paper to push it over onto each side to make sure it's all squared off nicely.
12) With a sharp knife, slice the block into about 1/3 inch slices; as you cut a slice, transfer it to a cookie sheet, adjusting the shape with your hands (slicing may tend to squash the squares slightly). Once all slices have been placed on the sheet, chill the sheet while you prepare the other half of the dough.
13) Once the second cookie sheet is ready, take the first sheet out of the refrigerator and place it in the oven. Bake for around 15 minutes, until cookies begin to turn golden.
14) Bake second sheet the same way. Makes around 3 dozen cookies.

Index

Made in the USA
Middletown, DE
29 May 2020